other books by Michael Green

I Believe in the Holy Spirit *(Eerdmans)*
I Believe in Satan's Downfall *(Eerdmans)*
Evangelism in the Early Church *(Eerdmans)*
2 Peter and Jude *(Tyndale Commentary, Eerdmans)*
You Must Be Joking *(Tyndale)*
The Day Death Died *(IVP)*

EVANGELISM
Now & Then

MICHAEL GREEN

InterVarsity Press
Downers Grove
Illinois 60515

*InterVarsity Press is the book-publishing division of Inter-Varsity
Christian Fellowship, a student movement active on campus
at hundreds of universities, colleges and schools of nursing. For information
about local and regional activities, write IVCF, 233 Langdon St.,
Madison, WI 53703.*

*Distributed in Canada through InterVarsity Press, 1875 Leslie St., Unit 10,
Don Mills, Ontario M3B 2M5, Canada.*

*Except where the author has made his own translation, quotations
from the Bible are from the Revised Standard Version of the
Bible, copyrighted 1946, 1952, © 1971, 1973 by the Division of Christian
Education of the National Council of the Churches of Christ
in the USA, and used by permission.*

Cover illustration: Slug Signorino

ISBN 0-87784-394-5

Printed in the United States of America

Library of Congress Cataloging in Publication Data

Green, Michael, 1930-
    Evangelism, now and then.

    *1. Evangelistic work.   2. Evangelistic work–
History–Early church, ca. 30-600.   I. Title.*
BR 195.E9G72   1982   269'.2   82-14798
ISBN 0-87784-394-5

15	14	13	12	11	10	9	8	7	6	5	4	3	2	1
94	93	92	91	90	89	88	87	86	85	84	83	82		

For those who know Christ
and care about
those who do not

Contents

Preface

Learning from the first Christians

What, not another book about evangelism?

It would not be needed if Christians were putting first things first. Our forefathers in the faith were accused of 'turning the world upside down' with the good news they told people about Jesus (Acts 17:6). But in the Western world, at all events, Christianity is far from a revolutionary, exciting dissemination of good news. It is seen as being on the side of the status quo, the conservative, the bourgeois, the dull. There seems to be little 'news' about it, and what there is appears to be anything rather than 'good'. Yet that is what evangelism means! I doubt whether most Christians even guess that evangelism is the sharing of good news. And they certainly do not regard it as their business. That is where we differ so enormously from the early church, where every man and woman saw it as his task to bear witness to Jesus Christ by every means at his or her disposal. The Christians of New Testament days saw dynamic worship, together with bold and imaginative evangelism, as the twin purposes for which the church existed. They put first things first. With us, first things often come last. Worship is dull and predictable, dominated by clergy and choir, a duty rather than a joy. And evangelism—well, in many circles it is almost a dirty word.

Indeed, if, by a miracle, evangelism came back into the 'first things' category, it would probably fall on deaf ears, because the individual life or church life would in many instances be so different from what is proclaimed. And even when evangelism is energetically undertaken, it often suffers from three defects. The message preached is an emaciated abbreviation of the New Testament good news. The methods used are stereotyped. The after-care is negligible. And, to cap it all, the whole thing is a very human-centred operation, relying on efficiency and technique rather than the Holy Spirit of God. I have tried to take account of these tendencies in the present book, and also to deal as best I can with that greatest obstacle of all, our apathy.

I would like to express my gratitude to the United Methodist Church of the USA for inviting me to give the Denman Lectures on 'New Testament Foundations for Evangelism' at their Congress in Miami, January 1978. It was in these lectures, and many other addresses on evangelism in England, Africa and Australia, that this book had its origin.

If some readers wonder what is the difference between this and my larger book, *Evangelism in the Early Church*, the answer is simple. That was a book of scholarship and research. This is a book for those who wish to discover and apply the principles, motivation and methods of the early Christians to the contemporary scene. I have not, in fact, opened *Evangelism in the Early Church* while writing this book, though of course many of the same points will have been covered. But the treatment is entirely different. This book is written to encourage evangelism today in the light of what was done then. It is firmly anchored in the New Testament, particularly the Acts of the Apostles. It is equally firmly rooted in the present day, particularly in the experience of evangelism I have been privileged to share in, most recently in the church of St Aldate's, Oxford.

If you do not like the book, that is fine by me. Do not waste time denouncing it. Go and spread the good news in your own way. With the Spirit for mentor, and the Scriptures for guide, go and love people for Jesus' sake and tell people where that love comes from. Put first things first and 'tell people the good news, in season, out of season' (2 Tim. 4:2). For this

10

civilization is dying for lack of it. If we are Christians at all, then we are in the Good News business. There is no higher priority for the churches which have lost their way in ecumenism, restructuring, revision of worship and other necessary but introverted pursuits, than to heed Jesus Christ's last command, 'Go and make disciples of all nations.' And it is precisely in this area of making disciples that the first Christians have so much to teach us.

Michael Green
St Aldate's Church
Oxford

Chapter 1

The secret of their impact

When eleven men set out to evangelize the world, we may be permitted to wonder how on earth they did it. Within ten years of the death of Jesus the gospel about him had reached Alexandria and Antioch, the greatest cities in Africa and Asia respectively. Almost certainly it had reached Rome by that time: it was so notorious a movement in the capital city of the world that Christians could be made scapegoats by Nero for the Great Fire in AD 64. The message spread like wildfire throughout the whole Empire, and were it not for the persecuting tendencies of Domitian there would probably have been a Christian emperor by the end of the first century. As it was, the movement had to wait another 230 years for that; but already it had captivated a multiplicity of races and cultures within the Empire, already it had made great inroads into the aristocracy and among the intellectuals, already it had changed the lives of countless ordinary men and women. Evangelism was clearly a priority among those first followers of Jesus.

What is evangelism?

One of the best definitions derives from Archbishop William Temple. 'To evangelize is so to present Jesus Christ in the power of the Holy Spirit that men come to put their faith in God through him, to accept him as their Saviour and to serve him as their King in the fellowship of his Church.' That, and no less, is evangelism. It is a matter of the Christian community sharing good news of a Saviour with those who do not know him. After all, what did the earliest Christians have? Not much. They had no Board for Mission and Evangelism. They had no conferences or training courses on the subject. They had no fixed creed. They had no code of conduct that was very different from the Judaism from which they sprang. They had no ceremonial. They had no church buildings, no priests. They had merely the assurance that Jesus was the long awaited Deliverer, that he had died, risen and was even now in the place of power in the universe. They then told people about him. They engaged in evangelism. But let us look a little more closely, for evangelism can easily be confused with other things.

In the first place, evangelism is not the same as mission. Mission is a much broader term than evangelism. It speaks of the total impact of the church on society, while evangelism is more restricted, the passing on of the good news.

Evangelism is not individualistic. Although it can happen between two people, as one beggar tells another beggar where he may get bread, evangelism always brings people into a fellowship of those who have also found the living God through Christ.

Evangelism is not a system. There are plenty of encapsulated messages, three-point sermonettes, four spiritual laws, 'bridge diagrams', and the like, current in Christian circles. While these may at times be helpful tools in evangelism, they are a menace when they harden into systems. For our Lord is not a system; he is a person. And evangelism is bringing someone face to face with this person. It cannot be done by a system.

Evangelism is not an optional extra for those who like that kind of thing. It is not an acceptable pastime for the person who likes making a fool of himself on a soap box in the open air, or titillating his ego by addressing a large gathering in a public hall. Evangelism is sharing the good news of what God has done for us all. It is the sacred duty of every Christian.

14

Evangelism is not shallow. It is, of course, often regarded as shallow by those who don't do it, and by some who do. Indeed, a lot that passes by the name of evangelism *is* shallow. But that is not how it is meant to be. It is intended to be the good news of how God takes sinners and builds them into a new society which constitutes the first instalment of God's kingly rule in a rebel world. There is nothing shallow in that message and its implications. It affects the intellect, the outlook, the relationships—everything.

Evangelism is not the task of the ordained ministry alone. It is not primarily their task at all. They are meant to preach and teach the faith, but by the very nature of things they are not in such close contact with agnostics as most members of their churches are from Monday to Saturday. There is no hint among ancient records that the early church saw evangelism as the task of the leadership alone. All were called to pass on the good news. It was too good to leave to the professionals.

Evangelism is not finding pew fodder. Sometimes when a church has tried everything else—in vain—it comes reluctantly round to the idea that if it is to stay in business it had better resign itself to an evangelistic campaign. If evangelism is anything other than the spontaneous outworking of the fire Christ has lit within, it will ring false and achieve nothing.

Evangelism is not man-made propaganda. God is involved in it. God the Father got involved when he sent his only Son. Jesus Christ deemed it such a priority that he made it the subject of his last command. The Holy Spirit was specifically given to equip the church for bearing witness. Evangelism is the outworking of the love of God in a fallen world. It is no man-made opiate.

What is more, evangelism is neither Christian proclamation alone nor Christian presence alone. It is both. There has been a disastrous tendency for some Christians to concentrate on proclaiming the gospel without showing it; so to emphasize the preaching that the feeding, the healing, the educating and the liberating fall into the background. In reaction, those who have concentrated on a 'social gospel' have been content to get among people and embrace them with the arms of Christ's love without bearing any overt witness to the one in whose name they do it. The very idea of separating the spiritual from the social gospel does despite to the New Testament. Jesus went about doing good and preaching the good news of the kingdom. His followers must aim for the same balance. There is only one gospel—of a God who reaches people in their need, rescues them, builds them into a new society, and is concerned with every aspect of their lives in this world and the next. This message must be both proclaimed and lived out. Presence alone and proclamation alone are equally useless. The early Christians employed both. So must we.

Was evangelism easy for the first Christians?

When we consider the achievement in ancient society made by that small handful of disciples, it is tempting to suppose that somehow or other things must have been easier for them. After all, look at the advantages they had.

Their advantages

They had easy communications. Under the Roman Empire you could go from the Black Sea to the Bay of Biscay without a passport, without paying much in the way of taxes at ports, and without fear of molestation by pirates. Moreover, you had a marvellous network of Roman roads. Yes, that explains it. But wait a moment. How long does it take me to fly from Vancouver to Heathrow? Ten hours? There must have been more to it than good communications.

They had a common language. Greek was the *lingua franca* throughout the ancient world. Peter could preach in it on the day of Pentecost and everyone could understand him, whether they were Cretans, dwellers in Mesopotamia, visitors from Rome, or Arabs from Egypt. But have we not a *lingua franca* today? English will pass muster in much more than half the world. So far as language goes, it is as easy for us to evangelize as ever it was for the apostles.

They had the advantage of novelty. Yes, that must be it. Nobody had ever heard the gospel before, so of course they would be likely to swallow it at the first attempt. Or would they? Have you ever attempted to reach members of another faith with the good news of Jesus? Do they swallow it at the first attempt? Remember that all the first converts, not just the occasional odd one of them, were converts from another faith. If you feel that novelty is the key to evangelism, there are some billions of people in the world who have never heard of Jesus Christ, and millions of others to whom his name is just a swear word. Try out the novelty theory on them.

No, instead of deluding ourselves into thinking that if only we had lived in the first or second century we would have found this evangelism business a lot easier than we do, let us spare a thought for the difficulties under which they laboured.

Their difficulties

In the first place they were so few. Just eleven men and a handful of women to begin with. About the same size as the congregation of a really broken down mission hall in a village in the wilds.

What is more, they had no learning. They were ignorant fishermen. To be sure, they had a tax collector among them, even the odd mystic—and one or two who later proved unexpectedly good at languages and preaching. But to those trained either in the sophistication of Plato or the niceties of rabbinic Judaism they were indeed unlearned and ignorant men.

They were culturally deprived, too. Little if anything of the culture of antiquity had percolated down to them. Even the most cultured of them, Saul from that provincial university of Tarsus, did not rush up to the Parthenon when he got to Athens saying, 'At last I can see what I have read so much about.' Instead his heart was stirred within him when he saw the city so given up to idolatry. That was not my first reaction when I went to Athens. Was it yours?

They had no organization behind them, those early Christians. And they possessed few really competent preachers. Indeed, speaking to large numbers does not seem to have figured among their possibilities at all, after the initial

17

splash in Jerusalem which resulted in a pogrom after the death of Stephen. After all, Roman emperors were rather itchy about gatherings that might be construed as political. Did not even so enlightened an emperor as Trajan warn Pliny, his governor in Bithynia early in the second century, that he must not allow more than fifteen men to assemble for the innocent purpose of becoming the local fire brigade? It is hardly suprising that city-wide crusades were out, as far as the earliest evangelists were concerned.

As a matter of fact, it was even worse than this. The Christians were despised and hated by Jews and Gentiles alike. In the Graeco-Roman world they faced some of the most formidable barriers imaginable.

Barriers to reaching the pagans

There was the barrier of race. The world was divided into two opposing camps, Jews and Gentiles. The Romans had managed to weld their conquests into some sort of homogeneity despite the variety of their racial backgrounds. But the Jews resolutely refused to fit. They worshipped one God, not many—atheists, the pagans called them. They had funny habits like not eating pork, circumcising their boys, and wanting to be idle for one day in seven. The Romans never understood the Jews, but they learned to live with them and gave them an astonishing measure of privilege. But the Christians were neither fish nor fowl. They regarded themselves as a 'third race', neither Jew nor Gentile. And they lived that way. They brought together in this strange third race members of both societies in the ancient world and welded them into a unity.

There was also the barrier of class—the haves and the have-nots. The ancient world was even more class-ridden, in one sense, than Hinduism or British public life. It was the divide between master and man, slave-owner and slave. There was no way in which these two classes of mankind could relate on equal terms—until the arrival of the gospel of Jesus Christ.

There was the barrier of religious pluralism. Their society, like ours, was intensely pluralistic. It was the generally accepted view that all religions were as good as one another—the Romans had a charming way of discovering who the local gods were when they conquered a country, and then identifying them with members of the Graeco-Roman pantheon. They would gladly have been hospitable to Jesus and asked him to join the club if the Christians insisted on it: indeed, a pagan emperor at the end of the second century had a temple with five deities in it, one of whom was Jesus. And yet he persecuted Christians. Why? Because they were fiercely exclusive in their claims for Jesus. He was not one of the crowd of deities. He was the only, the incomparable. But there is no doubt that the ancients faced as great a problem in the religious tolerance and pluralism of their day as we do in the contemporary climate.

There was the barrier of decadence in society. The Roman world in the first century was disfigured by lust, greed and cruelty to a massive degree. The first signs were appearing of the breakdown of society, signs with a curious parallel to our own day. Faced with the threat of a crumbling civilization, Christians not only grew and captured that civilization, but they outlasted it as they have outlasted every civilization since.

There was the barrier of political suspicion. Although they were not at first very active politically, their message cut at the heart of the most significant piece of propaganda that the politicians were putting over—the myth that Caesar was the supreme Lord, the august one, the initiator of the Golden Age. Christians refused to give Caesar the title of universal Lord. They refused to offer incense to his statue. Hence the suspicion in which they were held. It was as dangerous to be a member of a Christian church in first-century Rome as it is to be a member of a communist group in twentieth-century Washington. Moreover, there was a lot of talk about their disreputable ethics: Thyestian banquets and Oedipean morals. Did they not talk about loving their brothers and sisters and consuming someone's body and blood in a meal? You could not trust them. They were just the sort of antisocial people who might well burn Rome—which is why Nero found it convenient to blame them for the Fire which in all probability he himself started.

There was the barrier of cynicism. The society into which

19

Christianity was born was fed up with religion. To be sure, it was eaten up, like our own, with astrology and magic. But the heart had gone out of the old religion. You have only to read the *Satires* of Juvenal to see how contemptuous he is of the ancient Roman religion; and yet an inscription has recently turned up which shows that he himself was a priest! It is hard to beat that for cynicism. And today there are many within the Christian church who are its accredited ministers and yet publicly avow their disenchantment and unbelief—and the man in the street is rightly cynical. If those who are paid to be its ministers do not appear to believe the Christian faith, why should he bother his head about it?

There were considerable barriers to the success of Christianity in the Gentile world. Nor was it any easier among the Jews.

Problems in reaching the Jews

In the first place Christians were nobodies. Who had commissioned them? To what rabbinic school had they gone? Who among the leaders of the nation had turned to the new faith? No. The Establishment were solid against them. They hadn't a leg to stand on.

What is more, they did not keep the law of Israel. They ate with Gentiles, and non-Kosher meat at that. They neglected the sacred rite of circumcision; did not Genesis call down a curse on the head of any who refused to circumcise his sons? It seemed that these followers of Jesus disobeyed much of the Old Testament and laid exclusive claims to the rest. This could hardly be expected to go down well.

And on top of it all they proclaimed as Messiah a man who was an undoubted failure. Messianic speculation was both rife and somewhat vague in the first century, but the job certainly included ridding the country of Israel from its Roman overlords. Instead of doing that, Jesus had been executed by the Romans—at the instigation of the Jews. What impertinence to suggest he was the Messiah! Worse, it was blasphemy. The Old Testament made it perfectly plain that any man exposed to hang upon a tree was under the curse of God. Jesus was not only

20

a failure, but he rested under a curse. How could he possibly be the Messiah?

These were some of the formidable difficulties Christians faced as they sought to evangelize the Jews. And there was another thing that told against them. They were not committed to the defence of the State of Israel. Israel was as hard pressed then by the Romans, especially during the years AD 66–70, as she is now by the Arabs. And the Christians did nothing to support the nationalist cause; they dissociated themselves from it. Such people were beneath contempt in the eyes of the Jews.

So was it easier for them, this evangelizing business? I doubt it very much.

How did they succeed?

Undoubtedly the main secret of their impact was the outstanding change in their own lives. It showed up in a number of ways.

New people

Not to put too fine an edge on it, they were new people. This was the impression they gave at their first public appearance— they were so thrilled with their good news that they appeared to be drunk. The difference was that there was no hangover. The new quality of their living lasted, and it did not fail to strike the ancient world. There were failures of course, like Ananias and Sapphira, the rivalry between Paul and Peter, and the shambles in the Corinthian church. But for all that, the total impact was one of absolutely new life. They claimed that the cause for this was the fact that God's Holy Spirit had come to make his home in them. They lived their message.

Think of John, that 'Son of Thunder' who had once wanted to call down fire from heaven on a Samaritan village because of their lack of hospitality. He became the supreme apostle of love. Think of Peter, fickle and mercurial as he was. He became the man of rock on whose character and proclamation the Christian church was founded. One after another of these early

21

disciples was transformed into the likeness of the one they proclaimed. Incidentally this helps to explain a theological problem. It has often been remarked that there seems to be a deliberate parallelism between the acts of Peter and of Paul in the book of Acts. This is indeed the case, and should not be put down to the inventiveness of the author! Luke is at pains to point out that there is a deep similarity between Peter's life, Paul's life, Stephen's life and that of Jesus as recorded in the first volume of his work, the Gospel. It is the theme of transformation. Those who follow Jesus are gradually made like him. That is what Christianity is all about.

Paul, in his farewell to the Ephesian elders, says, 'You know how I have lived with you at all seasons.' His life was utterly transparent, and that was what gave power to his message. You cannot *pretend* to be a man of God. Our lives have got to manifest such a new quality, such marks of transformation, that people will be intrigued and will want to know why. Only then will they be impressed by the good news that we tell them.

As I think of those who come to faith in Christ through our church in Oxford, I believe the single greatest ingredient in the process is the changed lives of their friends. They know there is something different about them, and they are determined to find out what. Once our lives catch fire with Christ, then we will inevitably evangelize: we shall not need any instruction on techniques. After all, what excited explorer needs techniques in order to communicate his discoveries? If we are not thrilled with Christ and being changed by him, we can have all the techniques in the world and get nowhere.

Their dedication

Their dedication and willingness to obey, whatever the cost, is another of the notable marks of their changed lives. God gives his Holy Spirit to those who obey him (Acts 5:32), and they proved the truth of that. That is very near the heart of biblical 'holiness', and without it nobody reflects much of the Lord or attracts others to him. The Holy Spirit and holy obedience of life are integrally connected. Think of the Acts of the Apostles. In chapter 1 Jesus tells them to wait until the power of the

22

Spirit came upon them; then they would be his witnesses in ever widening circles—Jerusalem, Judea, Samaria and to the uttermost parts of the earth. They waited; they were filled; they went out to tell the good news in the power of the Spirit. In chapter 8 the Spirit tells Philip, a most successful evangelist, to leave a flourishing revival campaign in Samaria and go into the desert—where normally he could not expect to find anybody at all. He obeyed and went. And thus the Spirit of God was able to lead him to an Ethiopian eunuch of great influence whom he won for Christ. In chapter 9 Ananias is told to go and look up a notorious opponent of the faith, Saul of Tarsus. Ananias does not like the idea. He is afraid and reluctant. But he goes. And the Spirit of God is able to complete Paul's conversion and fill him with new life. Peter knows well enough that God has no use for Gentiles. The Spirit of God convinces him that he is to actually go and tell one of them about Jesus: he obeys and goes. The result is the conversion of Cornelius and his household and a notable breaking-out of the Spirit of God in Caesarea (chapter 10). In chapter 20 Paul himself is well aware that if he persists in his projected journey to Jerusalem he may well come to a sticky end. But he persists; he goes: and God's Spirit works mightily with him. We have all these examples before us of the link between obedience and the power of the Spirit in evangelism, but we do not heed them. God says we must humble ourselves and pray if we want to see his blessing; and we do not. God says that we must care for the poor and needy and not give preference to the rich: we choose to disobey. God says we must put him first if we want to see his power at work: and most, if not all of our gods come before him. We then wonder why we are powerless!

Their joyful sense of discovery

These people had found treasure, and they wanted others to know about it. These people were enthusiasts for Jesus Christ, and they shared that enthusiasm with others. These people were convinced that the meaning of the universe had been disclosed in the coming, the death and the resurrection of Jesus, and they could not keep quiet about it. They did not say, 'The church is a reasonable place to go on Sunday mornings—we have such lovely music,' but, 'Come, see one who told me all that I ever did,' or, 'We have found the Messiah—come and see.' They were witnesses, and acted like them. But how often do you find that in Christian circles today? Enthusiasm is suspect in this age of disenchantment. After all, everyone is entitled to his own opinion ... we do not want to be accused of proselytizing ... we must respect people's privacy! And so we hold our peace, and men and women around us, for whom Christ died and to whom he commissions us to go, hear nothing, and are quite oblivious of the fact (if fact it be) that we have found the greatest treasure in the world.

By contrast I think of a Jewish postgraduate at Oxford who had just heard of Jesus and put her trust in him. She told me that within ten days she had read the New Testament three times through, and could just feel God pouring his love into her. I think of some thirty young men and women in that university who during the past eight weeks have taken that same step of faith—not because anybody preached at them, but because Christian friends could not keep quiet about the good news of the Saviour, and they found themselves constrained by his love to begin the life of discipleship. That is how the gospel spread in the early days; that is how it spreads today when our enthusiasm for the Lord is allowed to be seen.

Their transparent love

But something else marked those early Christians. If it does not mark us, nobody is going to be very interested in what we say. It was their transparent love. There were great inequalities of wealth and opportunity among most people in antiquity, but it was not allowed to remain so among the Christians. Acts 4:32 tells us that the company of believers were of one heart and one soul. So much so that nobody laid personal claim to his possessions. They had everything in common. And with great power, we read, the apostles bore their witness to Jesus. Could it be otherwise when there was not a needy person among them? When those who had houses sold them and pooled the proceeds? Their loving fellowship broke down the natural

24

barriers between blacks and whites, between masters and slaves, between rich and poor, between those from Jewish and Greek backgrounds. They shared their goods, their meals, their worship—everything, as Justin put it, except their wives (the very area where the pagans were most willing to share, as he unkindly reminded them!) Think of those early disciples. What would Simon the Zealot and Matthew the tax collector have in common? They were political irreconcilables. The Zealots were committed to killing off the Romans, while the tax gatherers farmed the Romans' taxes for them. But the love of Jesus bound these two men together. Think of the brothers of Jesus who once upon a time did not believe in him and thought he was mad. There in the Acts we find them and his mother gathered with the disciples they had once scorned, in loving partnership and filled with the same Holy Spirit.

This love for the brethren is crucial. Without it there can be no effective evangelism. The world has to see in Christian circles a warmer, more accepting and caring fellowship than they can find anywhere else—and until they see that they are not going to be all that interested or impressed with God-talk.

Their endurance

Another astonishing feature of these early Christians was their endurance. Not merely of laughter and the cold shoulder, but of anxiety, persecution, prison and death. Think of the peace which marked the apostle Peter as he slept between his guards the night before his execution date! Think of Stephen kneeling with radiant face and praying for his murderers as the stones crashed into him and knocked the life out of him. Think of Paul and Silas lying in prison with their feet in the stocks and their backs lacerated from a gratuitous whipping. And what were they doing? Singing praises to God at midnight, if you please! That to me is a greater miracle than the timing of the earthquake which released them from the jail and led to the conversion of the jailer. That was the sort of endurance you could not quench. All you could do was kill these impossible men—and they went to their deaths singing. The ancient world knew all about stoicism, keeping a stiff upper lip in hard

25

times. But it did not begin to understand a man who could suffer and die with radiant joy and exultation.

Neither does the modern world understand that quality of endurance, but they notice it with awe. Three Ugandans accused of political crimes against General Amin were converted in prison. They grew in the power and love of the Holy Spirit. Then they were led out to die by public executioner. They urged Bishop Festo Kivengere, who was allowed there to encourage them, to go and tell the gospel to their executioners, while they bore witness joyfully to Christ before the crowd, and continued praising the God who had forgiven and would soon be receiving them right up till the moment when the shots rang out from the amazed firing squad. That story went round the country like wildfire. You cannot get the better of that quality of joyful endurance. Where it is shown, the church grows. As ever, the blood of the martyrs is seed.

Their concern for non-Christians

These early Christians had a tremendous concern for the 'lost'—those who had lost their way and were out of touch with the God the Christians knew in so personal a way. They really cared. Something of the intensity of that concern is shown in the earliest pages of the Acts. The apostles are told by the Jewish authorities to keep quiet; they refuse, politely, to do any such thing. They are clamped into prison: they get out, and after returning to their friends and engaging in deep and earnest prayer, they go to it again. In the streets, in the desert, in houses, before kings and governors, even when Paul is brought before the Emperor Nero himself, it is just the same story: they cannot keep quiet. They seek to persuade, to warn, to teach, to cajole others into that relationship with the risen Christ which has become the mainspring of their own lives, You can see how deeply it has burned into the soul of Paul from his farewell to the Ephesian elders, as recorded in Acts chapter 20. He maintains, 'I am innocent of the blood of all of you, for I did not shrink from declaring to you the whole counsel of God' (verses 26–27). He was thinking of Ezekiel's watchman.

Ezekiel had come to see himself as God's watchman on the walls of the city, who saw danger approaching. If he told them, and they did nothing about it, he had cleared himself. But if he did not tell them, the inhabitants of the city would perish, but their blood would be upon his head. Such was the burning sense of responsibility which Paul felt. People's blood would be on his head if he held back from telling them the good news of Jesus.

This was no peculiarity of Paul. The men who brought the gospel to Antioch (Acts 11:19ff.) must have been impelled by the same concern for others. Like Paul, they must have felt that 'if our gospel is hid, it is hid to those who are lost' (2 Cor. 4:3). So they made very sure that it was not hidden, but spoke not only to the Jews but 'to the Greeks also, preaching the Lord Jesus.' How could you do otherwise if, like Peter, you believed that 'there is salvation in no one else, for there is no other name under heaven given among men by which we must be saved' (Acts 4:12)?

Their priorities

One cannot fail to notice the priorities of those early Christians in this whole matter of sharing the faith with others. Although Acts 6:4 refers to the apostles and not to the general run of Christians, there can be little doubt that when the leaders devoted themselves 'to prayer and to the ministry of the word', the rank and file did likewise. Otherwise it would have been very difficult to see how uninstructed Christians could have argued out of the Old Testament Scriptures that the Messiah was Jesus. Do you know a church where the priority is prayer? Prayer in individual lives, in prayer cells, in half-nights of prayer? If you do, I can tell you one thing about that church. It will be evangelizing. In some way or other the good news of Jesus will be going out. Prayer is a priority in evangelism. Without it lives do not get changed however great the activism and however enthusiastic the proclamation. Most churches do not see church growth because they do not want it enough to pray for it.

It is much the same with the ministry of the Word. Do you

27

know churches where there is an honest, believing exposure to the Word of God? Where those who preach wrestle with Scripture; where individual Christians test what they hear by Scripture; where congregations regularly read the Bible devotionally and see it both as a guide for their lives and a powerful instrument with which to explain the faith to others? I can tell you one thing about such a church. They are very likely to be evangelizing. For 'the word of God is alive and powerful and sharper than any two-edged sword' (Heb. 4:12). It attracts people. It challenges people. It builds people up in the faith. It sends people out in mission. Living as we do in a hectic society where primacy is given to committee meetings, congresses, organization, mid-week meetings for senior citizens, church bazaars and the like, it is still incumbent upon us to make prayer and the ministry of the Word our priorities. That is still the way churches grow. I write these words in Vancouver. I have not been here for five years. And I am amazed at the way in which churches and Christian groupings which give a priority to Scripture and prayer have, during that period, been growing enormously both in range and impact and numbers. Those churches whose message is uncertain, those where prayer is not such a feature, are dwindling. It is a stark and inescapable contrast. As Paul put it, 'The weapons of our warfare are not worldly, but are mighty through God for pulling down strongholds' (2 Cor. 10:4) Those strongholds of unbelief and apathy do not fall to weapons less potent than prayer and the Word of God—and the people who turned the world upside down knew it.

Their power

I end this chapter with one of the most notable characteristics of all: the sheer power of these early missionaries. Jesus had promised them that they would receive power when the Holy Spirit came upon them, and that then they would be witnesses to him in Judea, Samaria and beyond. This power was there for all to see. It was life-changing power. It was character-transforming power: just imagine what must lie behind the bald statement that many of the congregation at Corinth had been idolaters, sexual perverts, thieves, drunkards, and robbers. 'Such were some of you. But you were washed, you were sanctified, you were justified in the name of the Lord Jesus Christ and in the Spirit of our God' (1 Cor. 6:11). Think of the moral and transforming power which lies behind such a throwaway allusion. People could see the power in these Christians: the power of new discovery, new moral resources, new enthusiasm. They could see the power of the healings and exorcisms that the early Christians performed.

It is much the same today. I know of many who have come to faith, some of them in Hindu countries, when one of their family has been suddenly healed in answer to prayer or has had a demonic and compulsive force cast out of their life. The sheer power of the Spirit in the lives of Christians is one of the most attractive magnets which draws people to Christ. 'Our gospel came to you not only in word, but also in power and in the Holy Spirit and with full conviction,' claims Paul (1 Thes. 1:5). People were not merely interested during his short three week campaign in Thessalonica: they were brought under conviction by the Spirit of God, and by that same Spirit they were converted. The word Paul uses for 'conviction' is an interesting one. It is *plērophoria*. It suggests a cup so full to the brim that it flows over. It suggests Christians so full of the Holy Spirit that when they were bumped into, it was not their own reactions of frustration or irritation that spilled out, but the gracious, lifegiving Spirit of God.

This trans-verbal communication is very powerful. It is the power of the Spirit given by the Lord to equip his servants for his task of mission. For the truth of the matter is that the Holy Spirit and witness-bearing go together. Is not that the meaning of Mark 13:10f.? The gospel must be preached to the pagans: the believers must do it: and the Holy Spirit would speak through them. But before he can do that he has to break us down. Break us of the pride and independence that come so naturally to us. Break us of the disobedience and lethargy that keep us silent in a day of good tidings. The Holy Spirit is not always a gentle zephyr; sometimes he is like a raging fire consuming all the rubbish in our lives, or a gale sweeping it

29

1 pride
independence
1 disobedience
lethargy

away. When he is allowed to have control in a church, in an individual life, then the possibilities for evangelism are unbounded. But only then.

In 1736 Bishop Butler wrote his *Analogy of Religion*. He was at that time the foremost philosopher in Britain, and he doubted whether anyone would succeed him as bishop because it seemed improbable to him that Christianity would survive his own lifetime. It was an age of utter unbelief, irreligion, self-centredness, not unlike our own day. Butler wrote, 'It has come to be taken for granted by many persons that Christianity is not so much a matter for enquiry, but is now at length discovered to be fictitious. Accordingly, they treated it as if in this present age this were an agreed point among all people of discernment, and nothing remained but to set it up as a prime subject for mirth and ridicule, as it were by way of reprisals for its having so long interrupted the pleasures of mankind.' By the end of Butler's life, so far from being swept aside, the good news of Jesus Christ as preached by Wesley and Whitefield had transformed the face of England. It could happen again.

Chapter 2

The quality of their church life

So far we have been looking at the qualities of character which those early Christians displayed. Now let us examine the quality of their church life. So often this is where the biggest problem in evangelism comes. The church presents a major stumbling block to a great many people looking in from the outside to see if Christianity has anything to say. 'Yes to God, No to the church' is their very understandable attitude. And I think you can see how widespread this is when you begin to ask non-churchgoers if they ever pray. I find to my amazement that lots of them pray regularly. But they never darken the doors of a church. After all, what's the point?

Nobody seems to have taken that attitude in the early days. The impact of the church as such was every bit as impressive as that of individuals. Indeed, it was more so, for their mutual interaction showed Christian love in action, and there is nothing more attractive than that. Nobody seems to have thought that the church was too dull, too respectable, too irrelevant—which is what they often think now. And they could be right. Which is why it may be worth looking at one of the churches in the Acts of the Apostles and seeing what insight it may give us into some of our present problems with the church. The story is found in Acts chapter 11.

Antioch on the Orontes was the capital of the rich, powerful Roman province of Syria. It ranked as the third city in the world, after Rome and Alexandria. It was multi-racial, militaristic, libertarian, wealthy and sex-mad. There were many Jews here, with special civic privileges of which they were jealously proud. Despite squeezing the maximum out of life, the citizens of Antioch seem not to have been entirely satisfied. Inscriptions have turned up to Lord Luck, Fate, Lord Serapis, Immortality, and so on. There were lots of horoscopes, and there was evidence of much astrology and use of magic.

It was in this difficult and yet curiously modern city that Christianity became a world faith. It was from here that the European bridgehead of Christian mission was launched. Had it not been for Antioch, Christianity might have remained a subculture of Judaism. Instead, it became a counter-culture, and survived both the disintegration of Judaism and the fall of the Roman Empire.

We live in a day when Christianity tends by most of the West to be regarded not as counter-culture, not as salt in the midst of a disintegrating society, but rather as a pious subculture for those who will sacrifice their minds and conform their behaviour in the hope that there may, after this life is over, be pie in the sky. A private cult, and at heart a selfish one. Maybe the Christian church has sunk to that in much of Western civilization. No significant influence in politics, thought, futurology, commerce, ideology, education or ethics. No readily distinguishable lifestyle apart from the curious habit of congregating in a large and chilly building once a week—or month.

At Antioch, in contrast, the church was seen to be a radical alternative, a counter-culture, a third race which was neither paganism nor Judaism. They did not make this impression because of the backing of the Establishment: there was none. Nor because of clerical brilliance: they were all lay people. Nor because they examined the problems of church growth in depth with a visiting guru at a congress. They succeeded because they were God's counter-culture. Almost every aspect of this radical alternative to the normal ways of life in Antioch must have been very costly. I doubt if we in our day can possibly

34

have effective evangelism without a costly revolution in church life, priorities and attitudes. Nor should we expect it.

Here was a church devoted to every-member ministry

The first thing we learn about the founding of this remarkable church should stop us in our tracks. Nobody singled it out as a prime target for church growth. Nobody sent a mission there. It happened almost by mistake! Christian folk, very ordinary folk, who had found Jerusalem too hot to hold them after the death of Stephen, left home and wandered from town to town up the Phoenician seaboard until they came to Antioch. They naturally chattered constantly to all they met about the wonderful new thing that had happened: God's Messiah, so long expected, had actually come, had been put to death, had risen, and people could come to know him. This information they restricted to the Messiah's people, the Jews. But as they reflected on the breadth of their leader Stephen's vision, they must have asked themselves why they should restrict themselves to Jews alone, since Jesus' death had universal significance. So they began telling other people, Greeks (11:20); and they found a ready welcome for their message. Were not the people of Antioch looking for satisfaction? They could do with good news. Were they not looking for deliverance from frustration, bondage to sexual orgies, bad relationships, the mad quest for wealth, and the grip of demonic powers? These wandering peasants told them that deliverance was possible for them through God's own Son, Jesus. And in a city where we know they worshipped many 'lords', the lordship of Jesus was an important part of the cost of discipleship. Such was their approach, it would seem, and before long there was a church consisting of both Jewish and Gentile adherents. A complete new advance in Christian witness had been brought about because a handful of Christians on holiday could not keep quiet about the Lord.

It is not until church members have the enthusiasm to speak to their friends and acquaintances about Jesus that anybody will

35

really believe we have got good news to tell. The respectability barrier, the clerical barrier must go down, if the church is to become credible again. It can be done. I think of a church where we once took a mission. It was a rather traditional Catholic Church of England congregation. The result of the mission was not only that many people there came to acknowledge and rejoice in the lordship of Jesus, but that they themselves could not keep quiet about him. Many of those who were converted in the first week had led someone else to the Lord by the second, and the work continues to grow. I think of a friend in Sri Lanka who often preaches on the streets, and has a regular trickle of Buddhist converts as a result. On May morning in Oxford when there are some 10,000 people on the streets by 6 o'clock to see the festivities, you will find Christians taking the opportunity to tell passers-by of the lordship of Jesus. Likewise in many a student residence and family home the good news is chatted over a cup of coffee late at night.

But this is the exception rather than the rule. If we are to see a widespread explosion of lay witness there has to be revolution in the churches. Revolution in the attitudes of the clergy: they must cease to see themselves as the only agents in mission. Revolution in congregational understanding: they must see that witness-bearing in some shape or form is the responsibility of all Christians. Revolution in church activities, to enable training to be done and people to be freed from trivial inward-looking activities in order to be the 'society for the benefit of non-members' which the church was designed to be. Training is vital. In our own church we have a fifteen-week training course followed by a three-week visitation in a nearby parish, comprising weeknight home meetings and Sunday preaching, one occasion of which is specifically evangelistic. The members of the course take the home meetings, speak in the services and help enquirers to faith. Needless to say this enormously strengthens the concept of every-member ministry within the church. Members find that they can do it, and that there is no joy greater than helping others to faith.

The biggest difficulty is normally to get a church to think evangelistically and actually desire growth. Many churches want everything to continue cosily just as it always has. That is not what the church is for! I think of a church I know in Singapore which has very different ideas of church life. A couple in the congregation are urged to prepare to buy or rent a flat in a nearby high-rise block, as it nears completion. They do, and move in with the first residents. They then go round and invite everyone to church. 'Church, where is that?' they are asked. 'In our flat, number 126,' is the reply. I saw one such 'church' which has sixty regularly worshipping there on Sundays, and a cluster of mid-week cells for prayer, study and mutual care. This was the spirit of which those who evangelized Antioch were made. We need more like them.

Here was a church which cared

They cared about new believers

Barnabas, that great encourager, was imported, and he did a lot to establish the new Christians, exhorting them 'to remain faithful to the Lord with steadfast purpose' (11:23). The after-care side of evangelism is greatly neglected these days, and this is shameful. God does not bring babes to birth only in order to have them frozen or starved. Perhaps the reason why many churches see so few conversions is because they are not prepared to put themselves out in after-care like this. Some churches, however, are developing a system of nurture groups, where batches of new Christians meet weekly for two months or so in order to get settled in the basics of the Christian life. A couple of 'Barnabases' are put in charge of the group, and not only do they teach and encourage, but the group soon becomes in many ways its own pastor, through the friendships, mutual encouragement and questioning, praying and reading the Scriptures together. Each night takes a different theme, dealing with one of the major aspects of Christian belief and behaviour. The group leader will teach, handle questions, and then encourage members to say how things have gone during the past week. Next they turn to a passage of the Bible related to the theme, discuss it and learn to pick thoughts from it,

37

before ending with short prayers from everybody. In this way members grow fast and reliably. It is an aspect of caring which the Antioch Christians knew very well, but on which most modern churches are very weak. How long ago did Wesley's class meetings go out of fashion?

They cared about the hungry and poor

Verse 28 shows a remarkable man with prophetic gifts, Agabus, coming into their assembly and telling of a famine that would hit the Christians in Jersualem. It so happens that we have independent testimony to this event, which took place in the late 40s. But to me the reaction of Antioch is more interesting than the problem at Jerusalem, which was probably due to an agricultural sabbatical year (one in seven was left fallow by Old Testament law) accentuated by the pooling and sharing of capital as practised by the early Christians at Jerusalem. Antioch could have said, 'We are not too keen on the theology and Judaistic emphases of these Christians at Jerusalem.' They could have said, 'That will teach them some economics: those who live off capital rather than income always run into trouble.' They said neither, but showed their love and care for their brethren by raising a handsome subscription and sending it to them in their hour of need.

It is this sort of practical caring which makes such an impact for the gospel. Until fairly recently I gather that there has been little or no response to the gospel among the Masai, a fierce Kenyan tribe of warrior nomads. But now there is a lively Christian church there. And much of the breakthrough has been due to the loving practical assistance in times of drought and danger afforded by their traditional enemies, the Kikuyu. Unless a deep, loving, practical care for the poor in their predicament is shown, the mere proclaiming of good news will be useless. I have just met an American pastor who spent some years working among the hundreds of prostitutes in Seoul in the latter stages of the Vietnam war. Scores of them were led to Christ, but not before he had identified with them in their felt needs for finding new employment, support of their illegitimate children and so forth. There can be no possible split between a social and spiritual gospel. They belong together, and without both elements the good news of Jesus will not get across.

They cared about those who had never heard the gospel

This is a notable feature of the Antioch church. Not only did they talk to the Greeks about Jesus, the poor lost Greeks who had never heard of him. They remained outward-looking, and cared enough about the regions beyond to be willing to have two of their greatest leaders, Paul and Barnabas, go out on the first missionary journey to reach as many of them as possible. You do not suffer the loss of two of your most gifted leaders for the sake of people you have never seen unless you care a great deal. It was in all these three respects a caring church. That sort of church wins and holds converts.

Here was a church where fellowship was real

This point stands out in strong relief. For it was in Antioch that for the first time Jewish and Gentile believers sat down and ate together as a matter both of principle and of habit. It is hard for us to sense how significant this was. Suffice it to say that both Jew and Greek regarded the other as unworthy of his spit! To sit down and eat together was revolutionary. It shows the quality of the fellowship that they were not willing to reverse this agreement when the heavies from Jerusalem came and leaned on them. Fellowship was more important than taboo.

Another sidelight on the quality of fellowship in this church is afforded by the names of the leadership in Antioch (13:1). They had Barnabas, a Cypriot landowner and Levite; Simeon, nicknamed 'the swarthy', who was clearly black; Lucius from Cyrene in North Africa, who was probably black too; Manaen, one of the intimates of the Herod family, and therefore very much an aristocrat; and a fiery intellectual from Tarsus by the name of Saul. I do not imagine it was very easy for this lot to live together in peace. But they must have achieved it. Otherwise their joint leadership would not have been possible. It is clear

39

that fellowship was a deep reality in Antioch. It transcended the barriers of race, colour, background and education. It spoke volumes.

Now this quality of fellowship has got to be seen among us if anybody is going to believe our words about reconciliation. God will not use our churches in evangelism if they are rent with division, backbiting, resentment and cold relationships between members. The fellowship of the church which evangelizes has got to be hotter than anywhere else in town. Did not Jesus give us a new commandment that we should love one another as he loves us? And how did he love us? Sacrificially and totally. That is the quality of love he expects to see in churches between the members. He commanded this sort of love. He prayed for it in his great high-priestly prayer. He died to make it possible by breaking down the middle wall of partition between Jew and Gentile. He sent his Holy Spirit to grow in our loveless lives the beautiful fruit of love.

Recently our church welcomed a group called the Sacred Dance Group. They used dance as a vehicle of worship, and this was very impressive. But even more impressive was the love they so clearly had for one another. This touched and challenged people deeply.

I think of a conference in New Zealand where a friend of mine took a Marxist whom he knew well. It was a missionary conference and it really came alive in worship and a loving sense of joint belonging to the Lord. This man was amazed. For all his experience of Communist cell groups he said that he had never experienced any fellowship like this before. That is what ought to happen when Christians gather; too often it does not.

I recall an Australian bishop telling me of his visits to a stone-age tribe in Indonesia where the gospel had just taken root. He saw them carrying twelve pigs up the hill. He asked the reason, and this was what emerged. There were two tribes in the area, hostile to one another. A young man in one tribe had gone to bed with a girl in the other tribe. Her tribal head was furious and demanded the death penalty. The young man was a Christian. He had sinned grievously. But the brethren in that tribe backed him up to the hilt. They showed the hostile

40

chieftain how repentant he was, and they pleaded for his life. Eventually the chief agreed to accept instead twelve pigs. The Christian group there did not possess twelve pigs; they were valuable and not easily acquired. But they scratched around and shared costs and denied themselves until they had raised the means to get twelve pigs, and they were just carrying them up the hill to the other tribe when the bishop arrived. They loved an erring member of their fellowship enough to do that! No wonder the gospel spread like wildfire in that tribe.

Here was a church where leadership was shared

Shared leadership

In a church like Antioch you might expect to find a bishop; you would certainly expect to find a dynamic minister and an assistant or two. You find nothing of the sort. Instead there were five men of different race, colour and education who formed the leadership. We do not even know which of them chaired the meetings. Theirs was a corporate leadership. Of course it would have been much easier to operate a pyramidal model, such as most churches have. But a shared leadership is much more effective. It preserves the congregation from the peculiarities of one man. It mobilizes a variety of skills and gifts. It provides a forum for lively debate and earnest prayer. The men at Antioch believed in it. I think we should listen to them.

Some years ago I was appointed head of a theological college, and inherited a pyramidal structure with the principal, inevitably, at the top. When I left six years later we had worked our way through to a team leadership. All matters of policy were hammered out among us in prayerful discussion. We pulled no punches, but loved one another even when we thought some of us were talking rubbish! When we could not agree the way ahead we did not vote, but deferred the matter until we came to a common mind. The leadership was shared, and it paid handsomely. It costs a lot, of course—the humility to listen to one another and learn from one another, the deep

41

commitment and loyalty to one another, the willingness to pray on when the answer does not win general acceptance. But it is worth it.

I find that this principle is perfectly possible to operate in a parish. We do in fact operate it in my parish. All matters of policy come before the Staff Meeting or the Standing Committee, and we discuss and work and pray until we come to a common mind. This involvement of a team in decision-making preserves us from idiosyncracies, from the errors that one man would not have foreseen, and from imbalance. It could make a lot of difference in the building up and outreach of many a local church. The very way in which the leadership loved and trusted one another would be an eloquent demonstration of the gospel proclaimed in the pulpit. Why do so many churches remain in effect one-man-bands? Is the minister afraid of having colleagues? Is the congregation afraid to get involved? This could not have been said of the Antioch church.

Shared type of leadership

But notice another thing. They did not merely have shared leadership at Antioch, remarkable as this was; they had a shared type of ministry. We read that the leadership comprised prophets and teachers. Now it would be hard to find more uncomfortable bedfellows than that. The prophet is always tending to move on instinct; you never know what the man is going to do next. And the teacher is painfully predictable. To use contemporary language, the prophet is 'charismatic' and the teacher is not. This is one of the hottest issues in a number of churches of all denominations all over the world at the moment. Antioch solved it by having both types represented in the leadership. How wise they were! This meant that the worship combined the warm spirituality of the charismatics and the balanced teaching ministry of the teachers.

How rarely is that balance found in a modern church, but what a power it is when the combination comes off. It is tragic to me when 'charismatic' Christians write off as second-class

42

Christians the men who could so deepen their understanding
of the faith; and when 'non-charismatics' fear what the
'charismatics' bring—the very elements of life, expectancy,
and vibrant sense of the reality of God which most churches
could do with. There was no such divide at Antioch. Nor need
there be in our own day. I have twice worked in teams where
both emphases were represented, and it is not only possible but
exceedingly beneficial to hold the two in tension. It is a most
constructive tension and I would never by choice go back to a
monochrome pattern. I am quite certain that the combination
is a great attraction in proclaiming and demonstrating the
good news.

Here was a church where worship was dynamic

Just imagine it. The Antioch Christians are at worship (13:2).
They are concentrating on the Lord, adoring him. The Greek
suggests that they were 'holding liturgy' to the Lord. They were
serious about it, so serious that they gave themselves to
fasting. Suddenly, the Holy Spirit guided one of the congregation to get up in their midst and deliver a prophecy—a direct
word from God for their situation. It was a remarkable
message: 'Set apart for me Barnabas and Saul for the work to
which I have called them.' Most remarkable of all, they acted
on that revelation. They fasted again, prayed, and sent the two
men off on the epoch-making first missionary journey, as
we call it.

Unity and variety

A number of things are very striking in that brief cameo. They
were united in worship: that was the first thing. The attractive
power of a congregation at worship is hard to exaggerate. The
unity, the intensity, the variety of the worship should raise
questions in the mind of the stranger which it is the task of the
preaching to explain. I have just been to worship in a church
where the following elements found a place: wholehearted
singing to the Lord, leading off into singing in tongues; the use

of a singing group, small orchestra, dance group and a couple doing a dramatic representation of a broken marriage, with a most skilful potter at work commenting on remoulding their lives while throwing two pots on the wheel to illustrate the theme. It was an astonishingly varied offering of worship, and it made a wonderful preparation for the preaching. The whole service took three and a half hours. But nobody seemed to mind. They were worshipping the Lord, and were quite taken up in it. What a contrast to many a dull, unimaginative, repetitive church service!

Fasting and prayer

There are other noteworthy features in this description of the worship at Antioch. They fasted. That is most unfashionable these days. It used to be said that the Anglo-Catholics drank and the evangelicals ate—but fasting seems to have gone out for both of them. To fast means that we say to the Lord, 'Look, I am willing to do without sleep, food, sex, and other things that I deem important because I want to be 100% for you at this time.' It is a mark of our seriousness with God.

Along with it goes the emphasis on prayer. To be sure, you might expect them to do that in a worship service! But this was no mere recital of petitions. The whole congregation was waiting on the Lord in a silence that could be felt. It was into this context that the Spirit could speak. It is in prayer that we are formed and remade, and it is through prayer that God is free to reach and use us. If we do things for God without praying he cannot afford the risk of allowing us to succeed. For we would get proud, and would be hardened in our conviction that activism, not dependence on God, is the way for Christians to serve their Lord. I believe there is no single lesson we need to learn more earnestly in the whole work of evangelism than prayer. If we prayed for God to thrust out labourers into the harvest; if we prayed that he would show us what he wanted our church to do; if we prayed in support of evangelism and missionary work instead of giving lip-service to it—we should see great advance. On the whole, we are very prayerless Christians. That is one reason why we are so ineffective.

44

I shall never forget learning this lesson afresh. The occasion was a mission in the University of Cambridge, and I was leading it. Large numbers were packing the Guildhall every night, but few were professing conversion. Many Christians in Cambridge mentioned that they found it very hard to pray. So did I. On the penultimate night of the mission I did not sleep very much, and I think that was fairly general among the Christian community. We had finally begun to give prayer its place. Back in Nottingham at St John's, where I was on the staff, somebody had a vision that night. It was of me standing between the trenches in No Man's Land during the first world war. There were soldiers in our trenches who were supposed to be supplying covering fire. Instead they were playing cards. That vision drove people in St John's to prayer, and a prayer vigil was kept in a room apart all that day. In the evening in Cambridge some 800 students stayed to an explanation of the way to Christ after the final talk, and scores of them committed themselves to our Lord. It certainly taught me a lesson about the link between prayer and evangelism.

Order, spontaneity and silence

Another feature of the worship that fascinates me at Antioch is the interplay between order, silence and spontaneity, which is not difficult to detect. On the one hand they were conducting liturgy to the Lord; on the other, they were open enough to the Holy Spirit to allow and receive a prophecy made quite spontaneously by one of their members. At least, that is how I assume they became aware of the Spirit's call to Barnabas and Saul. If not, it is even more amazing that they should all have come to the same conclusion silently on their own as they prayed. Surely this interplay of structure in worship, silence, and expectancy that God might break in in some unexpected way should mark a lively congregation? But the Holy Spirit would have an awful job forcing his way into the services of most churches! They are utterly predictable and all organized beforehand. I am not pleading for lack of preparation. I am pleading for such a sensitivity to God among those who lead worship, that it should not be impossible for God's Holy Spirit

45

to get something across to the people should he so desire. In our own congregation we are feeling our way towards this once a month, with an informal evening service where an outline structure is provided, but time is spent in silent waiting upon God and members of the congregation are asked to contribute as they are led, in song, scripture, prayer needs, or some word from God for the people. These services are invariably packed, and the worship, fellowship and expectancy are high. We are gradually learning to combine structure with flexibility under the Spirit of God—but we have a long way to go before we reach the sensitivity of Antioch.

Obedience

There is a final feature about their worship which has something to teach us. They obeyed. Once convinced that God wanted Saul and Barnabas overseas they were prepared to part with these trusted leaders. Obedience is part of worship, and a much neglected part. There is an entertaining and most gifted pastor in Argentina, Juan Carlos Ortiz, who tends to preach on the same theme for some time. One of his congregation asked him, 'Why do you preach to us the same message Sunday after Sunday?' The reply was unanswerable. 'Because you do not obey God on this matter. As soon as the congregation begins to obey, I will preach about something else!' There is far too much of the atmosphere of the club about much Sunday worship. When we begin to wait on God unitedly, expect him to make his will known to us, and determine to allow that time of worship to affect our lives in obedience during the ensuing week, then we may expect to see people being converted by the power of the worship alone. For they will see that God is in our midst. And they will want to find him too. This is no starry-eyed optimism on my part. I have seen it happen in our own congregation as people have been converted by the sheer sense of God in the place without any evangelistic preaching. Alas, it has not happened very often ...

Here was a church which looked beyond itself

Antioch itself was a missionary situation. It was a young church which owed its origin to informal missionaries. It could well have argued that they had plenty to do in Antioch, and could not bother about anything beyond their borders. But that is not how a church behaves when sharing good news is a way of life. As we have seen, they were devoted to every-member ministry in their midst. They expected every member to take some active initiative for Jesus. It seemed, therefore, only natural to show that concern more widely. Hence their support of the Jerusalem Christians when the famine struck. Hence their readiness to send Paul and Barnabas on the missionary journey to Cyprus and South Asia Minor.

Their visionary outreach is really remarkable. I doubt if they would have even listened to the Spirit on the missionary call had they not already been thinking about the folk who needed to hear the gospel not only in Antioch but beyond. But they did have the interest, and when the call came they heeded it. Just imagine the sacrifice involved in allowing two of their most gifted teachers and leaders to depart on some mad excursion, nor knowing where they would go or whether they would ever see them again. 'What a waste to let them go off into the wilds: the heathen are quite happy as they are,' one Antioch Christian might have said. 'In any case we need them here. Doesn't Antioch need converting?' another might have rejoined. We do not know if they had such modern attitudes. If they did, they were overruled. For the congregation at large and Paul and Barnabas in particular were glad to follow what they were convinced was a call from the Lord which could not properly be gainsaid or neglected.

Is there not an important lesson here? We shall be fired to evangelism in our own locality in proportion as we are willing to neglect our own needs and look to needier places overseas which we can support. It is the church which waters others that is herself watered. But how few churches seem to believe this. There is no real missionary concern. Nobody has gone out from that church for years to the foreign field. There is no expectation that anybody will. There is no feeling that it matters—and yet from all over the world pleas are coming, heart-rending pleas, for personnel to support and serve as fellow labourers with the national church. If the plea is heard, the tendency is to say, 'Well, we give to a missionary society. Is that not enough?' or, 'We can't send Bill—he's needed here,' or, 'These other countries have got their own religion, haven't they? What right have we got to interfere?' If the Antioch church had pursued such policies we in Western Europe might still have been strangers to the good news of Jesus Christ.

My small experience goes to support the claim that once a church begins to become concerned about mission overseas, and starts to pray for labourers to be thrust forth into the harvest, before long somebody offers. And then another, and another. And those who go find a fulfilment that they rarely find in the home country. And those who stay have a real prayer concern for them—did they not go out from their own church? I find that the congregation will give generously to support one of their own midst who has gone out; and that this is a much better method than giving vaguely to the general funds of a missionary society. I find that members of the church write to them and send them gifts. I find that slides and news letters come back, and are shown at the prayer meeting and in fellowship groups. And the overseas church and the home church are alike enriched and edified.

I believe that this sort of enrichment across the cultures and across the barriers of nationality is so important that it is a key function in evangelism. Not long ago a group of converted Auca Indians came and took a series of meetings in Britain. More recently several East African bishops led a mission in different parts of the country. What a splendid way in which to show that the gospel is for all, and that the movement is so far from being one way (from America and Britain towards the third world) that the third world needs to be our teacher in the realm of evangelism.

I believe that most churches could do a great deal to encourage this outward look, even in a small way, by taking groups of the congregation to engage in mission, even if only for one service or for a weekend in another nearby church. I hardly ever accept a speaking invitation nowadays unless I can bring a team with me. In this way many of the congregation get a taste of outreach and are prepared for the bigger challenges that God may bring their way either personally or as a church.

There are some churches which have the resources to release one or two of their members or even their staff for a limited assignment overseas from time to time. I happen to belong to such a church, and two of us go regularly on overseas trips, but only after the Standing Committee of the church has had the conviction that it is right for us to go; and only when leaders of the congregation have laid hands on us and sent us out in their name; and only as the congregation undertake to pray for us when we have gone, and gather to see slides and hear news when we return. In this way we all glimpse something of the catholicity of the church of God—one church throughout the world, in which we have the privilege to be a small part. That was what the Antioch church learnt so clearly. They heard the call. They supported it. They laid hands on Saul and Barnabas. They prayed for them. No doubt they financed them. And they gathered to hear their news and to share in prayer and praise for all God had done with and through them. Antioch was a church which looked beyond itself.

Here was a church where thoughtful teaching was prominent

Lest we should gain the impression that with their instant chattering of the faith and impulsive missionary initiatives the Antioch Christians were all heart and no head, consider the thoughtful brand of Christianity they represent. It was a group of Hellenists that led them to Christ in the first instance, followers of the martyred Stephen. They spoke Greek, they thought Greek, and whereas the Jewish Christians saw God primarily as the God of the law, the temple and Israel, these people thought otherwise. They realized that the temple was overshadowed by the presence of God in Christ; that the customs delivered by Moses (food laws, sabbath and circumcision) could not measure up to Christian freedom in the age of the Spirit. The centre of their vision was the risen Jesus. He was supreme in the whole world. He was the Lord Jesus. It is interesting that it was these Hellenists who were driven out by Judaism while the conservative Christians of Jerusalem were given a peaceful ride: the twelve, James the Just and the rest apparently stayed on unmolested in the holy city. In other words, the Jews themselves distinguished between these Hellenist extremists (with their revolutionary views about the outsider, the law and public worship) and the Palestinian Christians (the Establishment folk, who seemed merely a harmless set of devout people).

It is salutary to remember that the future lay with these Hellenists, not with the conservatives. They translated the gospel into the terms which secular people of the day understood. They had a big enough conception of Jesus to be emancipated from the shackles of attempting only what had been done before. They saw static religion as a betrayal of the God of Abraham: the climactic indictment of Stephen's speech is that Solomon built him a house (Acts 7:47). They realized that God does not live in buildings but in people. They saw the sphere for the gospel not in the straightjacket of Palestinian Judaism but in the secular Roman Empire. It was in this spirit that they came to Antioch.

They continued to think once they had got there. How were you to commend the lordship of Jesus in this situation? Should Jews and Greeks eat together? What should be the limits of Christian caring? What about mission? How about training? These were the issues with which they struggled. The record stresses how seriously they took teaching the Christian faith. So much so that they imported Barnabas, and he brought Saul from Tarsus, and 'for a whole year they met with the church, and taught a large company of people' (11:26). We have reference to their teachers in 13:1 and a further extended spell of teaching followed the first missionary journey. It was taken seriously.

Very few churches take teaching seriously. As a result church members do not even begin to suspect there is a Christian mind on the major issues of the day—let alone adopt it. The underlying Christian understanding in most congregations is puerile, the unbelief vast, the conformity to the world's standards almost complete. The lack of critique of contemporary culture by the churches, the lack of concern over major social and political themes, the lack of wrestling with the contents of the gospel and how to share it, the absence of training courses and study programmes is appalling. Scripture speaks of a new birth, a new mind and a new society. Many churches are antipathetic to all three, and many of those who are most enthusiastic for the first are weakest on the other two. 'Transformation' is the key to most ideologies these days—a very biblical key. But do we use it?

I write from a summer school in Vancouver. 200 people from all walks of life have given up three or six weeks of their holiday in order to come and do a demanding series of study courses in Christian education: systematic theology, the world of the Old Testament, a study of the New Testament from Hebrews to Revelation, Christian theology in the context of human cultures, contemporary literature, medical ethics, the doctrine of the church, music in church, and the family in secular society. When the church treats teaching seriously there will be no lack of takers. Whereas a programme of this sort is beyond most churches, courses of sermons, a proper use of the mid-week meeting, an all-age Sunday school, training courses in public speaking and counselling, could be within the competence of many a church or small group of churches, and the result would be an increase in Christians really thinking about their faith and applying it to life. This could dispel the idea that Christians are naive and keep their religion in one compartment and the rest of their lives in a quite different one. How we need the burning heart and the cool head of the Antioch church! It is a powerful combination in evangelism.

Here was a church with one overmastering passion

We are told that it is in Antioch that the believers were for the

51

first time called Christians (11:26). This is highly significant. They did not call themselves Christians, you will notice. They were called it by others. It was a nickname.

The nickname was based, no doubt, on the widely disseminated 'household' of the Emperor. These men were known as 'Augustiani', because they were employed by Augustus, loyal and devoted to him. Well, it seemed reasonable to the citizens of Antioch to coin a word for the followers of the Way in their midst. They used the 'Augustiani' as a model. So 'Christiani' came into being, Christ's people, sent by him, loyal and devoted to him.

I wonder what led the Antiochenes to coin this word for the believers in their midst? It must have been because they kept speaking of Christ, kept working for Christ, kept trying to please Christ, acting as they thought Christ would have acted. What a testimony this bears to the faithfulness and wholehearted dedication of the early church in Antioch. They were consumed with a passion for Jesus Christ. He was their Lord, he was their first love; nothing else was so important to them. And the pagans knew it.

I suppose that this is the most crucial mark of any church when we are considering the matter of evangelism. If people have really found good news, they will always be majoring on it; they will always come back to tell of Jesus and his love. They will seek to make him Lord in every quarter of their lives. They will by speech and behaviour remind people whose they are and whom they serve. That is what it was like at Antioch. And when a good proportion of the members of any church are passionately in love with Jesus like this, then inevitably God adds converts. For there is nothing so attractive in the world as a life where Jesus is dominant. And those in whom he is dominant will not be ashamed to give the glory where it is due, and so to speak of their Lord, however haltingly and shyly. That is the supreme secret of an evangelistic church: one that has a single passion—only Jesus.

How is it we never go out together anymore dear....?

Chapter 3

The shape of their message

In these days when there is such a lot of dispute about
evangelism, it would be marvellous if we could ask those early
Christians some of the questions which perplex us. Granted
the quality of their corporate and individual lives, which bore
such eloquent testimony to the power of Jesus Christ, how did
they actually go about it when people asked them what they
were so excited about? I propose, therefore, in this chapter, to
look at four questions which certainly are in the minds of
contemporary Christians, and to which the early missionaries
seem to me to give a fairly decisive answer.

What is your perspective?

The Christian world has been rather polarised between two
extremes. One stresses the importance of preaching the gospel
to all and sundry. The other stresses the importance of the cup
of cold water in the name of Christ. Social and spiritual gospels
are not alternatives. they belong together.

When I was an undergraduate the Student Christian
Movement in the universities seemed to stress the social
gospel; the Inter-Varsity Fellowship represented the need for
personal salvation and verbal proclamation. In this particular
instance doctrinal convictions separated the two bodies, and a
great deal of mutual distrust and suspicion made any cross-

fertilization hard. But clearly, evangelism and social care belong together. It would be unthinkable that Jesus should have preached but not healed: or that he should have fed the multitude but given no indication of where the Bread of Life might be found. The two were inseparable.

George Hoffman discovered this when he was on the staff of *Crusade* magazine. He wondered whether evangelical Christians who were unenthusiastic about the value of famine relief agencies where the name of Jesus Christ was muted, might be interested in supporting a project where Christian proclamation and presence went together. The result was TEAR Fund, which within a few years has become one of the largest relief organizations in the Western world. A Christian organization which met social and spiritual needs at the same time caught and still catches the imagination of the Christian public, and evokes support not only in generous giving but sacrificial going.

Alan Walker, an Australian Methodist whose influence is world wide, has some trenchant remarks on this subject.

'The argument for a social Christianity runs something like this. Open a coffee shop and show the youth you are with it: serve endless cups of coffee with a smile: but make no mention of Jesus Christ. Run a "togetherness" event to defeat the loneliness of society, but plan no moment of proclamation, thereby ensuring that the event will reflect the culture and values of society round about. Begin a Counselling centre, aid people to become adjusted to themselves, their neighbours, their environment; but say nothing about their most fundamental need of all, adjustment and reconciliation to God. Start a community aid service, or open an old folks' home, but be content if creature comforts are met . . .'

As he acutely comments, no adequate community of Christians has yet emerged from the 'Christian presence' approach. Presence without proclamation is a failure, and the early Christians were certainly not guilty of it. You have only to glance through the pages of the Acts to see how ludicrous they would have regarded any such suggestion. The Christian movement would never have got off the ground had the earliest missionaries not been devoted to proclamation, just as they were to caring. Like Jesus, they regarded the two as indivisible.

Look down Christian history. Is it not true that the great forward movements of the church have been through the proclamation of the good news? Peter, Paul, Origen, Savonarola, Luther, Wesley, Whitefield, Jonathan Edwards, William Temple, Martin Luther King and the others moved the hearts of people through telling them of Jesus. But in each case there was an inescapable social implication in their proclamation. It is a matter of root and fruit. The only gospel worth having is rooted in an encounter with the living God which has as its necessary fruit and stamp of authenticity a passionate concern for people's needs and involvement in their struggles and aspirations.

The Letter to Philemon could never have been written had spiritual and social gospel, proclamation and presence methods been considered alternative options in the early church. They were no options! Paul led Philemon, a rich Colossian land-owner, to Christ. Philemon's runaway slave, in the humorous providence of God, landed up in the same prison as Paul and was soundly converted by him. The result had immediate social consequences. First Onesimus' conscience got to work; he felt bad about the money he had stolen from his master and knew he must return, even though it might involve death. Second, Paul wrote to Philemon on behalf of his new convert; not only does he beg Philemon to treat Onesimus in love as a fellow man and fellow Christian, but he hints that he should release him. And Philemon himself, we may assume, lays aside the anger and resentment which he would naturally hold against a runaway thief, and begins to love him—in a fellowship of master and slave that was exceedingly rare in antiquity. The social and spiritual parameters of the gospel cannot be separated.

What do you talk about?

Granted that they made a point of proclaiming something, what was its main thrust? This is a question that is relevant in an age when those who do talk about the faith vary enormously in what they say. I find that a great many emphasize 'my experience of God'.

This seems to be both foolish and sickening. Foolish, because people's experience differs a great deal. Sickening, because it points to me, not Christ. In the early days, we find that Christians did no such thing. They bore witness to Jesus.

Martyria, 'witness', is one of the great New Testament concepts. It comes constantly in the Acts. And it does not mean washing my spiritual linen in public, but telling people in my own words about Jesus and his resurrection. The emphasis is all on him, and the additive is my own humble assertion (based on having tasted and seen that the Lord is real) that Jesus is living and available and life-changing. In the New Testament this is always the prime sense of the word 'witness'. *Martyria* meant telling of Jesus, in the first instance; later it came to mean dying for Jesus, as is evident from our word 'martyr'.

It is of course true, as Dr James Dunn has stressed in his book *Unity and Diversity in the New Testament*, that there was a phenomenal difference in the ways in which different New Testament witnesses spoke of Jesus. There was, and we are all the richer for the diversity. But, as he is careful to point out, the greatest point of coherence in it all is the person of Jesus. They all spoke about him, from whatever angle they came. We could profitably learn from Philip, one of the Seven, who 'went down to a city of Samaria and proclaimed to them the Christ,' and, when speaking to an African in his chariot, 'opened his mouth, . . . and told him the good news of Jesus' (Acts 8:5, 35). Jesus is the one to talk about—not the weather or the problem of pain.

What are you looking for?

Here again there is some measure of polarization in Christian circles, into what I might call the 'decision' people and the 'process' people. Some stress the need for sudden conversion; others dislike the word intensely, and think of the Christian life as a process of becoming. But the early Christians would have considered this a very strange debate. They knew nothing of a decison that did not lead into discipleship and integration within a loving Christian community. Equally they would have found it impossible to understand the idea of Christian becoming without Christian beginning; it would have been as odd as life without birth. An acquaintance of mine makes a speciality of asking people how they came to understand the power of God in their lives: and over 90% of those questioned replied in terms of a moment rather than a process: but that moment led on to a lifetime of dedicated service to Jesus Christ. 'Born to Grow' was the catch phrase of the United Methodist Church Congress in Miami, January 1978. That precisely expresses the balance. If you are born you must grow: but to grow you need to have been born. The two emphases, as so often, are complementary.

It is worth reflecting for a moment on the conversion of Saul of Tarsus. This is not only the most famous conversion in Christian history, but the most bizarre. Those who dislike the idea of conversion often baulk at it; after all, are they expected to hear a voice from heaven and have scales falling from their blind eyes? Of course not. These are the frills, not the essentials of Saul's conversion. But in a fascinating place in 1 Timothy 1:16 Paul goes so far as to say that his conversion is the pattern for us all. How could this be?

There are four elements in Saul's becoming a Christian as recorded in Acts 9, which do in fact apply to us all. Whenever the good news of Jesus is proclaimed and responded to these four elements will be found. They are four essentials in every conversion.

It touched his conscience

'Saul, Saul, why do you persecute me?' asked the Voice (Acts 9:4), and many manuscripts add the proverb: 'It is hard for you to kick against the goad.' Saul had struggled with a bad

59

conscience ever since he held the clothes of those who stoned Stephen to death. He had a shrewd idea that he was persecuting Love as he drove Christians to their death. Behind the Christians themselves he was launching the attack of his hurt pride against a shadowy figure of whom he was only half aware. And now that figure had caught up with him. He knew it in his conscience.

This always happens, does it not? I do not mean that everybody comes to faith through the gateway of an accusing conscience. There are many gateways into Christ. But I do mean this. Whenever someone comes face to face with Christ, he is driven to the conviction that he is not worthy, and that Jesus is. One of the surest signs of a genuine conversion is a conscience that has become sensitive.

It opened his mind

'Who are you, Lord?' . . . 'I am Jesus' (verse 5). Saul, the proud Pharisee who had so stumbled at the crucified Jesus, now realizes that he is exalted to the place of 'Lord'. Jesus, and Lord—in those two words you see to the heart of the early Christian confession, and the essence of the Christian proclamation. The condemned, crucified peasant has the right to the name Adonai, Lord; the word used of God himself in the Old Testament. It is hardly surprising that the two words became the centrepiece of the short creed used by early Christians at their baptism: 'Jesus is Lord.'

This is not a very full doctrinal statement. Not nearly as full as a great many Christians would like to make it. But it sufficed to bring Saul into the faith. I do not see how it is possible to become a Christian on less doctrine than this. Unless I believe that the Jesus who came into this world, who died for me upon the cross, is the risen one who has the right to share God's name and throne—then it is hard to see any way in which I could probably be called a Christian. But it is important to notice that Saul does not appear to have been convinced of a lot more facts about Jesus than this. We in our turn have no right to expect of people at the turning point in their lives more than this minimal understanding of who Jesus is and what he has

60

done. This is enough to begin with: as Paul's letters indicate, this early knowledge tends to expand!

In verse 6 there are some words which are not contained in all the manuscripts. They tell us that Paul, 'trembling and astonished' replied to the Lord. These words speak of his emotional turmoil, and it is perhaps symbolic that their place in the manuscript tradition is uncertain. Because it is abundantly clear that whereas some people's initial commitment to Christ is accompanied by much emotion, with others there is none whatsoever. Conversion has nothing to do with feelings, any more than the marriage service has: in both, however, they are not unusual! I have known people to turn to Christ in genuine and lasting conversion, and they have done so as coolly as if they were deciding to wear a particular suit of clothes. I have seen others, as John Wesley did, in his day, who fell down and writhed upon the floor as they faced their Maker and Redeemer for the first time. The emotional content is variable and unimportant. The heart of the matter is the will.

It reached his will

Saul acknowledged the Lordship of Jesus. Saul allowed himself to go where Jesus indicated, into the city of Damascus. This is what signalized the essence of his conversion. The Lord had 'converted' or turned to Saul in a most gracious approach, and showed his willingness to receive him. Now Saul turns or 'converts' to God, and grasps the proffered hand in awesome gratitude at such unexpected grace and in total dedication. His will was the vital thing, and so it is in every conversion. Incidentally, this explains to some degree the phenomenon of false conversion, the person who has 'tried it all and it does not work'. My experience with many such people is that they have not tried it all. What they have done is confuse emotion with commitment, or ardour with discipleship. They may have made some sort of overt response in days gone by, but on inspection they will agree that there was no wholehearted turning to God and handing over to him of their whole future, as Saul did. The citadel of their will remained unstormed, and they were not converted.

It changed his life

'He is a chosen vessel unto me, to bear my name before the Gentiles' (verse 15). The whole subsequent direction and quality of Saul's life was transformed by this encounter with the living Christ. The changes were staggering, and some of them are evident from this very passage.

We find him praying (verse 11). He had said prayers three times a day, if not more, for as long as he could remember. But now he is making contact with God: 'Behold, he is praying.' This is one of the earliest and surest marks of new life. The convert begins to find prayer a reality. Of course, for the Holy Spirit is now within him, enabling him as a tiny baby in the Father's house to lisp, 'Abba, dear Father' (Rom. 8:15).

We find him looking for and revelling in Christian company (verse 19). That is another common early mark of discipleship. Christian company, which had seemed so unattractive, now appears as both a necessity and a joy.

Another mark of the new life is Saul's desire to share what he had discovered about Christ with others. 'In the synagogues immediately he proclaimed Jesus' (verse 20). We find this one of the most frequent signs of conversion in the lives of new Christians in our church. Most of them are seeking to share the faith with their friends inside a few days—without anybody suggesting it to them. It is the natural outworking of what God works within.

Acts chapter 9 is instructive in further ways. It presents us in Saul of Tarsus with a man who is anxious to grow. He is not satisfied with where he has got, but is straining forward. 'He increased all the more in strength' (verse 22). As in physical, so in spiritual life, appetite is one of the surest signs of health.

He becomes increasingly bold. He is willing to face opposition and court mockery for his change of position, both from within and from without the circle of his new companions (verses 21, 23). That is a sign of new life. So is his willingness to accept help from others. Previously this proud, confident man would much rather have given help than receive it. But now we find him willing to be ministered to by Ananias, fed and taught by the Christians, and rescued from a riot by them as they lowered him over the wall to safety in a basket. No-one can be a Christian without letting Christ serve him. This usually has the effect of opening a person up to receive help from others. I recall one young man telling me that he disliked and despised the Christians in his university until he came face to face with Christ. The very next day he went to them and asked them to help him with his new faith, There was a new openness to receive, as well as to give. Christ had softened up the heart.

Yes, conversion produces a changed life. If there is no change, there has been no conversion. But even as I write these words I am uneasy about them. The descriptive words we have been using, 'decision', 'process', 'conversion' are all man-centred. They are quite inadequate to describe the way in which Saul's encounter with God is meant to be a model to subsequent generations. Perhaps the most important thing which happened to him, and which should be the hallmark of all of us, is that the Holy Spirit of God came and entered his life. He was baptized and filled with the Holy Spirit (9:17–18). The apostolic age expected 'new birth' or 'a new creation' in their converts, for the person who had been a stranger to the Spirit became his shrine. The regenerative power of God enters the life of those who turn to him in repentance and faith; and through the regenerate life of individuals God sets out to regenerate the world.

What do you say?

I wonder what you would say if some friends, impressed by the difference Christ seemed to make to members of your congregation or yourself, came and asked how they could find what you have got. Where would you begin? Or would you be tongue-tied, and turn them over to somebody more experienced? That might on some occasions be appropriate. But since they have come to you, I think it is probable that they would want to hear from you. Perhaps those early Christians could once again provide us with a clue? I see five elements coming time and again in their preaching of the good news in the Acts—and the many sermons recorded enable us to get a good idea of the shape of their message.

They emphasized a word

It is a strange phrase, but one that echoes throughout the Acts. 'The word' seems to be the heart of what they communicated. Wherever they went these early Christians spread the word (8:4). For eighteen months at Corinth Paul was gripped by the word (18:5). It was the same at Ephesus (19:10). So much so that when Luke means us to understand that the church expands he tells us that the word grows. So it was in Judea (6:7), Samaria (8:14) in the first missionary journey (13:44) and in the campaigns in Asia (19:20). No wonder the Twelve made it a priority (6:4). No wonder they commended their converts to it (20:32).

Does someone believe? It is because the word leads to faith (8:4ff.). Does someone receive the Spirit? The word enables him to do so (10:44). Does someone become a Christian? It is the word he receives (17:11). Is someone a counterfeit Christian? It is because he has no part in the word (8:21).

It really would be hard to exaggerate the importance they placed on 'the word'. It means, of course, their proclamation of Jesus on the basis of the Old Testament. And so they claim that their message is not merely the word of men but the word of God which changes lives (1 Thes. 2:13). The word of God is the prime agency in the spread of the good news.

The question then faces us: do you believe that the message about Jesus preached by the apostles and embedded in the New Testament is in fact God's word to man? If you do, you will bring people face to face with it at every turn. C. S. Lewis is enjoying a popularity unparalleled among modern advocates of the Christian faith. Why is this? Because after his conversion from atheism to Christ he bent his massive intellect so to understand the word of God that he could expand it with clarity and power. He got gripped by the word. His teaching is simply and unashamedly New Testament teaching. It is applied with

64

freshness and charm, with sensitivity and insight. Herein lies its power.

I believe that the churches have to get back to Scripture if there is to be widespread evangelism in our world. People are not embarrassed if you turn them to the Bible. So long as you do not make any fuss about whether they believe it or not, and merely expose them to its pages, this will seem a thoroughly reputable procedure—as indeed it is. What better way of examining any subject than to get back to the primary source?

We would be wise to store away in our memories certain key verses or passages from Scripture, or we may well prove to be the blind leading the blind when we try to help others. The early Christians memorized Scripture. It is clear from their quotation of the Old Testament that they had a strong preference for particular passages—Psalm 110 was the most favoured of all. Moreover C. H. Dodd, one of the greatest New Testament scholars this century, has shown that there was a basic pattern underlying the early preaching of the gospel. It was a rough outline, which of course was not slavishly followed, but provided a basic structure for the preachers to memorize and use as they thought fit. The pattern they used ran something like this (consult Dodd's book *The Apostolic Preaching and its Developments* for the details). 'The age of fulfilment has dawned, as the scriptures foretold. God has sent his Messiah, Jesus. He died in shame upon a cross. God raised him again from the tomb. He is now Lord, at God's right hand. The proof of this is the Holy Spirit whose effects you see. This Jesus will come again at the end of history. Repent, believe and be baptized.'

Not a bad basic structure. It is a good deal more comprehensive than the 'three-point' potted evangel which many purvey; or the 'four spiritual laws'; or the 'five things God wants you to know'. How we prostitute the good news by oversimplifying it! The early Christians really gave themselves to studying and thinking out how they would proclaim this 'word'. They neither turned the gospel into a system nor made it shallow and simplistic. They knew that the good news was like a sea: a child could paddle in its shallows, but a giraffe would be out of its depth before long. How could it be otherwise with God? So we find the early preachers taking lots of trouble. No five-minute sermonette and challenge for them! Paul could argue all day with the Jewish leaders (28:23). He could talk till Eutychus fell asleep and out of the window— then, after the interruption, resume till dawn (20:7–11). He could hire the lecture hall of Tyrannus during the hot dead hours in the middle of the day and fill it with eager enquirers (19:9).

John Stott has drawn attention to the variety of words used to describe the early evangelists in their handling of the 'word'. They got to grips with it in earnest. 'To testify' is very frequent; so is 'to argue'; 'to clinch the discussion'; 'to debate'; 'to compare texts'; 'to proclaim good news'; 'to act the herald'; 'to teach'. They immersed themselves in that word which they proclaimed. We must do the same. It is not the churches which have left the biblical emphasis and perspective which are growing these days. It is the churches and para-church organizations for whom the Scriptures do embody God's word that are growing at a very great speed. This is an age of the relative, the slick: but people are hungry in their hearts for the truth of God, and as they are exposed to the 'word' of the New Testament, they find, as J. B. Phillips discovered when translating the Scriptures afresh, that these documents carry the ring of truth.

They spoke to a need

There was nothing rigid or unimaginative about their approach. They set out to discover the spiritual location of those to whom they spoke, and once they had assessed their need they related Jesus to that. They were, as we must be, bridges: rooted in the Scriptures and also in the contemporary situation and the needs of the particular individual or group with whom they were dealing. The Acts records an amazing flexibility of approach. Look at Philip dealing with the eunuch, a man in search of meaning, and scanning the prophet Isaiah to find some (8:30ff.). Look at Paul handling the very modern man, the proconsul Sergius Paulus, who was only interested in what really worked (13:7ff.). In Pisidian Antioch Paul spoke directly to the felt need of the citizens there: they knew God's law, and had a bad conscience because they were failing to keep it (13:39). When he got to Athens and found them frivolous, always playing with the latest novelty, Paul cut right through this shallowness by bringing them face to face with the judgment of God (unfashionable as it might seem) and with the historical resurrection of Jesus, the pledge of that future judgment's reality.

Or look at the way in which Stephen handled the regular churchgoers of official Judaism. He showed them in his speech how throughout the whole of their history God had been moving them on, and that by refusing to turn to Christ, the climax of God's revelation, they were in fact resisting the Spirit.

Sometimes they were shameless opportunists. I think of the Philippian jailer, terrified, flustered, wondering what way out of this situation would avail to let him save his skin and keep his job. Paul humourously takes his phrase 'be saved' in quite another sense, and leads the man to a security greater than he had dreamed possible.

Or think of the rather more extended approach which the early Christians took to the polytheism or atheism around them. (Incidentally, at heart both polytheism and atheism are the same). They did not talk about Christ and sin; to have done so would have been meaningless. They generally made a threefold approach, apparent in the account of Lystra (chapter 14), Athens (chapter 17), in the Letter to the Romans (chapter 1), and in Christian apologetic up till the fourth century. Indeed, it is still valid.

They spoke to the mind of the polytheist, and argued the existence of God, one Creator both of the world and mankind. He provides. He cares. In the past, unbelief may have been understandable; but not now God has shed such abundant light through Jesus Christ. No doubt they adduced the evidence for who Jesus was: his matchless teaching, his miracles, his quality of life, the prophecies pointing to him, his sacrificial death, his mighty resurrection, and the visible power and presence of his Spirit.

They also spoke to the heart of the polytheist. They laughed at the stories of the amours and battles of the gods as regaled by Homer and the poets. Scorn is a strong weapon, especially when the other person's heart supports your ridicule of the idols he somewhat ruefully puts first in his life.

Conscience, too, was their target. They set out to attack immorality, and show how wrong belief led to wrong conduct. They laid stress on man's accountability to the God he has spurned. They made clear the need for choice. In all these ways we see the early Christians discovering the needs of those they sought to reach, and only then relating Jesus Christ to them.

In today's world the hunger for freedom, the aimlessness of purpose, the quest for truth, the emptiness of existentialism, the pragmatism of science each require a different approach. It is up to us to row our boat round the island of a person's life until we discover where to land. I find that with a scientist, used to the empirical method, the wisest thing is not to argue with him about the pros and cons of believing in God, but to face him with evidence. That is what he is used to professionally. So give him a task to do: for instance, to explain the character of Jesus if he is not what he claims to be. Or ask him to give an alternative to the resurrection that can face critical investigation. Great numbers of scientists come to the Lord through examining the evidence critically, weighing it up, and then committing themselves to the Christian hypothesis on the strength of it—only to find that it works! That is precisely what they do in their academic studies.

But that would not be the way to handle a heartbroken widow, grieving over the death of her husband. She too needs to discover that Jesus is the resurrection and the life, but she will do so by feeling Christ's compassion through you, and seeing it in the story of the raising of Lazarus, rather than being driven to it by study of the evidence.

I think of an able existentialist whom the local students deemed impervious to the gospel. He came to Christ with joy and gratitude once he found himself understood. There was no need to talk to him about man's predicament and need (which the Christian students had been doing assiduously.) He was well aware of that. He needed to understand that faith was not a leap into the dark but into the light; that openness to the ultimate experience meant not self-destruction but the entry into a new dimension of being; supremely he needed to come into an I–Thou relationship with Jesus Christ. He did so, and became a fine Christian man. Like the early Christians, then, we must discover the need in the person we are talking with, and relate the good news, that many-splendoured thing, to his felt need.

They told of a person

No philosophy of life engaged their attention, no system of morals, but the living, loving person of Jesus. Him they proclaimed. Wherever you look in the early preaching of the good news, you cannot help being struck by their concentration on the person of Jesus. Jesus—the one who can still troubled consciences (13:39), the one who can fill an empty life (2:38), restore a paralysed man (3:6), exorcise a possessed girl (16:18), or rescue sailors in a storm (27:21ff.). Martin Luther once said that 'as we come to the cradle only in order to find the baby, so we come to the Scriptures only in order to find Christ'. It is the person of Jesus which attracts people; we must, therefore, keep the spotlight on him. Be Christ-centred, however flexible your presentation, if you want to follow the example of the earliest missionaries. Some aspects of what they considered important about Jesus might not come amiss.

They told of Jesus as fulfilment (2:16ff. and chapter 7 entire). Jesus is no merely contingent figure through whom God arbitrarily decrees salvation: all the Old Testament scriptures, and the whole history of salvation over millennia, point to him. The ideal no longer lies beyond man. The ideal has come, and his name is Jesus. People often think of Christianity as backward-looking, in an age when everybody else is looking to the future. It is our fault that they have got that impression. Jesus comes not so much in the past as at the mid-point of time, the right time; and he shows within the confines of a human life the answer to man's search for the best. I remember a university lecturer once coming up to me at the

69

end of a mission address and saying, 'Thank you. I teach English in this university. You have shown me how Jesus Christ is the fulfilment of the existentialist quest.' I think of a Jewess whom I took through some of the major prophecies in the Old Testament: she saw how those scriptures fitted Christ in a way they fitted nobody else, and she put her trust in Israel's Messiah—and is now a missionary overseas.

They told of Jesus the man; Jesus of Nazareth was 'a man approved, attested to you by God with mighty works and wonders and signs' (2:22). I wonder if we would regard this stress on the humanity of Jesus as a gross understatement? Maybe, as in 17:31, we would major on his 'otherness', his oneness with the Father? Like the early Christians, however, we must hold the right balance in our proclamation of Jesus. In the past the church has given the impression that Jesus is so entirely God that he is scarcely one of us. That, as some modern theologians are reminding us, is idolatry and blasphemy. It leads to a Jesus-worship which gives as little room to the Father as to the Holy Spirit. It also accounts for the tendency at a popular level, particularly in Catholic countries, to regard Jesus as, for all practical purposes, so far out of reach that you need the assistance of St Christopher or the Blessed Virgin to get his ear!

On the other hand, if we see Jesus as too exclusively a 'man for others' and no more, there is no salvation, no way from us to God. We are driven to paradox whenever we seriously consider the person of Jesus. He is both divine and human. He is the bridge that is anchored firmly on our side of the river, and yet reaches equally firmly to God's side. In this way alone can he be an adequate representation of the invisible God. In this way alone can he bring needy folk like us into a right relation with God. A bridge that does not reach both sides of the river is not a bridge, but a folly. The earliest evangelists instinctively kept that balance. Read a really earthy Gospel like Mark's which begins, 'The beginning of the gospel of Jesus Christ the Son of God', and then proceeds to show how firmly Jesus is one of us! Or consider how Peter complements Acts 2:22 ('a man attested to you by God') with 2:33ff. Instinctive trinitarian that he is, he points to the resurrection of Jesus and continues, 'Having received from the Father the promise of the Holy Spirit, he has poured out this which you see and hear'—and then comes our old friend, Psalm 110:1, to stress that this 'man attested by God' is none other than the Lord who shares the throne of Almighty God. The balance is superb.

They told of Jesus crucified. Unlike some Christians they did not seem to stress, at any rate universally, any particular doctrine of the atonement. But they did make it plain that their hearers were implicated in the human guilt of putting Christ on the cross: it was their fault that he hung there. What is more, they spoke of this crucified and risen Jesus offering people forgiveness (2:38). They sometimes thought of him as the passover lamb (20:28), sometimes as the Suffering Servant (8:35), and sometimes as the one exposed on the wooden stake of Deuteronomy 21:22, the place of the curse (*e.g.* Acts 5:30). This rare word, *xylon*, means 'wood' and is used of the cross in only a few New Testament passages which allude to Deuteronomy 21:22. Paul makes the meaning very clear in Galatians 3:10, 13. He was struggling to understand how God's great Messiah could have ended up not only in the place of impotence but of cursing: had not Deuteronomy proclaimed, 'Cursed be every one who hangs on a tree'? And then he saw it. Christ had indeed endured the place of cursing; but the curse he bore was not for any misdeeds of his own but for us—we who have failed to keep God's law and are therefore liable to its penalties (Gal. 3:10). In varied ways like these the early Christians tried to help people see what Jesus had done for them on Calvary. They were clear that the cross did not save anyone. It was Jesus who saved, but a Jesus who had gone to the cross for sinners. We might profitably emulate their flexibility, Christ-centredness and reserve.

They told of Jesus risen. The Lord who broke the shackles of the grave was the one they all knew: 'we all are witnesses' (2:32). This confident assertion both of Christ's resurrection and of their personal relationship with him runs right through the Acts. It comes in every evangelistic address recorded there. It is a major theme. I wonder if our contemporaries would say

71

the same of us? Are we known as the people who are always indicating that Jesus is not dead but alive, and that we know him? The churches which are growing these days are churches like that.

I remember a few years ago seeing written all over the walls of Oxford, 'Ché lives.' He didn't, of course. Ché Guevara, the self-sacrificing leader, was dead, even though his ideology lived on. The messianic myth, for such it was, proved fragile at its most crucial point. The man was dead and did not rise. But nowadays many thousands of people are turning to Christ in Bolivia where Ché used to operate. And on the walls of Oxford I see a different legend: 'Jesus lives.'

They told of Jesus reigning. Embodiment as he was of crucified love, he now shared the throne of God (2:34). The very universe is dominated by a love we have spurned but which will not let us go. That is the principle which people at their best most admire—in the mother sacrificing herself for her children, or the captain for his ship. And that is the principle which God rates most highly. I think it is important for us in evangelism to help people to escape from their childhood image of 'gentle Jesus meek and mild' and realize that in him they are confronting the very essence of the universe, a God who gives and gives, whatever our response— or lack of it. It is to him, enthroned on high, that we are bidden to give our loyal allegiance. The only lasting thing in the universe is this self-abandoning love. Unless we are touched by it and begin to show it, we are bound for chaos.

Finally, they told of a contemporary Jesus. He is no mere figure of long ago, but our contemporary. That is how they understood the Holy Spirit (2:33). He is the presence of Jesus for today, released from the limitations of a physical body. The early Christians seem to have recognized from the outset that their experience of the Spirit was a continuation of their experience of Jesus. The Spirit was the means by which their Master kept them company. No longer was he the fitful, subpersonal manifestation of the naked might of God (as so often in the Old Testament days), but God's mighty presence brought to us in Jesus. 'The Spirit', they maintained, 'has come and changed our lives; he can do as much for any of you.' Had all Christians seeking to evangelize given this stress on the person and work of the third person of the Trinity, there would have been less talk of the 'baptism with the Spirit' as a second initiatory experience and less confusion over the gifts and graces of the Holy Spirit.

Such was the rounded picture of Jesus that they seem customarily to have presented. They have shown us the way.

They offered a gift

This was one of the most surprising elements in the early preaching. Most religions tell you of something you must do. This religion tells of something God has done, through Jesus on the cross. Acts 2:38 puts it very plainly. When his audience wanted to know what they should do in the light of Peter's preaching, he told them not to do anything at all, but to receive what God had done for them. He etches a picture of the Lord approaching them with two gifts in his hand. They could never deserve them; they could only accept them or reject them.

God proffers them the gift of forgiveness: complete cleansing and pardon, whatever they have done in the past. And this is possible because of what Jesus Christ achieved on the cross. In other words, forgiveness is nothing to do with merit or living a good life or being nice and helpful. How could these things buy God's favour? It took the cross to make possible man's full and free acceptance. The finished work of Calvary meant that 'through this man forgiveness of sins is proclaimed to you, and by him every one who believes is freed from everything from which you could not be freed by the law of Moses'. Grace is utterly free for us—but was infinitely costly to God.

God proffers us another gift, the Holy Spirit. In days of old he was confined to special people; perhaps a king or a prophet might expect to be filled from time to time by the Spirit of the Lord. But he was not generally available. Indeed in the centuries immediately before Christ, people had ceased to expect or claim the presence of the Spirit of God. He went out, they reckoned, with the last of the prophets. They had to

73

satisfy themselves at best with the *bat qol*, the 'daughter of the voice'.

But Jesus was the man full of the Spirit. Jesus was the last and greatest of the prophets. He not only embodied the Spirit of God in every way of which a human being was capable; he promised to dispense the Spirit to his followers. And on the day of Pentecost it began to happen. The Spirit of Jesus came upon the believers, making Jesus real to them and changing them into his likeness as he equipped them for the service of others and the proclamation of the good news.

And all of this was sheer gift! I wonder if most people outside the church today see Christianity as a gift? Do they not have the image of the church which is always appealing for money to mend its leaking roof, or do this or that improvement? Do they not see Christianity as a threat to their joys rather than the fulfilment of their being? Do they not see it as a dreary attempt to be good instead of a dynamic experience of the love and power of Jesus let loose in their lives? Have they any idea that God justifies the ungodly, the undeserving? Do they realize that it is not a question of grim duty but of generous gift? I doubt it. And to the extent that people fail to see this (whether they respond to it or not), we, Christ's followers, have been false witnesses to the good news.

They expected a response

Like their Master before them who changed the whole direction of people's lives as he looked into their eyes and said, 'Come, follow me,' the early missionaries never tired of challenging their hearers to accept the gift proffered to them, and to begin in earnest the life of following Jesus Christ.

They expressed it in different ways. Sometimes the thrust was to repent: sometimes to believe; sometimes to be baptized (Acts 2:38f.; 16:31). All three strands are connected. All three are necessary. They saw that people could not come to receive God's gifts with dirty hands. They needed to drop the mud with which they were playing and come with empty hands to be washed and receive. Repentance is not primarily an exercise in remorse about the past. It is an attitude of turning back to God:

74

a change of mind, resulting in a change of direction. It was to 'repentance towards God' as well as 'faith in our Lord Jesus Christ' that Paul urged his hearers (Acts 20:21). The basic human failure is not in our peccadilloes but in our relationship with God, ruptured through years, decades even, of rebellion and neglect. Repentance is the willingness to have this put right, and the determination to remove any hindrances on our side to its repair.

Faith has two sides, a cognitive and a volitional. It does involve some understanding, but not necessarily a great deal. To believe that in Jesus Christ God has done all that is needful to restore the broken relationship is, I suppose, the bare minimum intellectual content in faith. As we have seen, 'Jesus is Lord' seems to have been the earliest baptismal confession. It centres in *Jesus* the historical figure, and the meaning of the word is 'Yahweh saves'. So in making that confession the candidate is recognizing that through Jesus God is becoming his saviour. And *Lord* takes us back to Psalm 110:1, where Jesus is seen to fulfil the role of the 'Lord' who sits at God's right hand. Jesus is Saviour, Fulfiller and Lord. That intellectual framework will need to be enlarged throughout the years of a Christian's discipleship, but it all begins in those two words.

The other side of faith concerns the will, and this is the most important. When a meal is laid before me, I act in faith. I have some (vague) idea of the ingredients: that is the cognitive side. But I know very well that unless that intellectual appreciation leads to action, and a very specific action at that, I shall never be satisfied by that plate of food. I must receive it. I must take it into myself. And it is an act of faith. I cannot be sure before I eat it that the food will not poison me. Such faith is well-grounded, normally, particularly when I know the one who provides the meal! In the case of Christian beginnings we can be very sure that the Father will not poison us. 'He who spared not his own Son, but delivered him up for us all, how shall he not with him freely give us all things?' (Rom. 8:32). How wise, then, to 'taste and see that the Lord is good. Happy is the man who puts his faith in him' (Ps. 34:8).

Baptism is the physical expression on our side (Rom. 6:1ff.)

75

of that repentance and faith. But it is also the sacrament of God's part in the whole transaction. Not only does it make over to us, like a will, all that Christ did for us upon the cross (without our co-operation or even consent): it symbolizes and may effect the outpouring of God's Holy Spirit in our lives. John baptized in water, but Jesus baptizes with the Holy Spirit, and it is impossible to be a Christian without having that Holy Spirit in your life. 'If anyone does not have the Spirit of God he is not a Christian.' So runs Romans 8:9. I do not want now to enter into the vexed relation between water baptism and baptism in the Holy Spirit. I have done that at length in *I Believe in the Holy Spirit*, chapter 8. The two are meant to belong together as the outside and the inside of the same thing. In practice they can and do happen at different times and in different orders. The point at issue here is that we need to respond to God's generosity by welcoming his Spirit into our lives and being publicly baptized into his allegiance. It take two to make a relationship. God approaches us with his arms held out in love, proffering us forgiveness for the past and his Holy Spirit as guardian of the present and pledge of the future. We have to make up our minds whether or not to say 'Yes' to his offer and challenge. That is why the demand for a response is an essential part of proclaiming the good news.

It is, of course, an area which most of us shun. We hate challenging people. It is not done. They might be annoyed, put off. They might say 'No', and then where should we be? Yes, we hate it, but it is absolutely necessary. For unless Christ is given access to the life he remains outside and cannot start his work of renewal. Unless it is taken and eaten, the meal does us no good! The act of will is essential.

Jesus told us that he intended to make us into fishers of men. Now, fishing happens to be my hobby. I know that when I get back in the evening after an expedition in search of trout, I will not impress the family who ask me, 'Daddy, how many did you catch?' if I have ruefully to reply, 'None, but I had several nibbles.' We are called not merely to influence people but to catch them. We cannot escape the role of gently urging them to claim personally what Christ has done for them.

Many have found the imagery of Revelation 3:20 and John 1:12 helpful in leading people to decision. The idea of welcoming the Saviour into the heart and life is readily understood and theologically accurate. It was this way of expressing things that particularly struck a chord with me. Others find the analogy of 'coming to Jesus' the most evocative: that, too, is thoroughly biblical (Mt. 11:28; Jn. 6:37). For others Paul's great concept of 'in Christ' makes most sense. I am not 'in Christ' by nature, but I can be grafted in, like a branch to a tree or a limb to a body. Only then do I begin to discover that 'if any man is in Christ, there is a new creation' (2 Cor. 5:17). There are plenty of other metaphors which the New Testament writers use to illuminate this experience. Accepting God's judicial acquittal is one which Paul loves: being adopted into God's family is another of his favourites (Rom. 8:15; Gal. 4:4–7). Being immersed in the Spirit, like ground long parched which is suddenly flooded, is another helpful picture (1 Cor. 12:13). In all of them the same main point is stressed: God's proffered gift of salvation has to be personally claimed and appropriated. Until it is, it will do us no good.

At this point it is essential to be very sensitive in dependence on the Holy Spirit. Sometimes the enquirer needs time to go away and reflect on the issues that have been made clear to him: sometimes he needs to be brought to decision. Only the Holy Spirit can show us which. When in doubt it is wiser to give the maximum room for decision, while reminding him to 'seek the Lord while he may be found, call upon him while he is near' (Is. 55:6). Factors which sometimes help to precipitate decision are first and foremost gratitude to Christ for all he has done; secondly, the need other people have of the gospel and our inability to commend anything we have not personally tasted; and thirdly, the folly of turning one's back on God's greatest gift.

But there are other factors making for indecision, and it is as well to be aware of them. *Confusion* is one: he may be confused about what he is supposed to do, and many not like to admit it to you after your eloquent explanation, in case you might be hurt. He may be confused about this whole area of personal religion, having seen it previously as a very formal and corporate affair. He may have unresolved *intellectual problems* like the credibility of the resurrection, the ability of 'good works' to bring someone to God, the problem of pain if God is good, and so forth. This is where your bookshelf and your patience come in! On the other hand he may simply be suffering from *lethargy*: why do today what you can comfortably put off till tomorrow? You will need to remind him that nothing worth while in life is ever achieved by the lethargic, and that lethargy looks very shoddy if the Christian story is true, and if God loves him enough to suffer Calvary. Most common of all you are likely to find *fear* underlying his delay. He is afraid it may not work, afraid he may not be able to keep it up, afraid of what his friends will say, and afraid of the future. These can each be simply met, but sensitivity and sympathy are needed. Fear is, after all, one of the strongest of our emotions and one to which we least easily own up. Fear that 'nothing may happen' is best dealt with by the promises of God. Fear about not being able to keep it up is best handled by showing that it is God's responsibility to keep us, ours to trust him to do so (1 Pet. 1:5). Fear of opposition is well founded: in some form or other, 'all who desire to live a godly life in Christ Jesus will be persecuted' (2 Tim. 3:12)—but what we have to face for Christ is nothing compared with what he faced for us, and most people are quick to see this. Fear about the future is no good reason for a person to hold back from entrusting his life to the only one who knows the future. The sheer logic of Romans 8:31–32 or the sheer comfort of Matthew 28:20 can be very helpful at this juncture.

When you have gently dealt with problems like these, it may be wise to ask your friend if he thinks he is ready to take the step of surrender to Christ as Lord. If he says 'No', then you need to find out whether it is something he does not understand or something he is not yet willing to do which is acting as a blockage—and move on from there accordingly. If he says 'Yes', ask him whether he would like to go away and sort it out with God on his own, or whether he would care to pray then and there in your presence and with your support. If he chooses to go off on his own, encourage him to come and see you when he has taken the step of faith, for 'if you confess with your lips that Jesus is Lord and believe in your heart that God raised him from the dead, you will be saved' (Rom. 10:9). If he prefers to stay with you, I generally find it helpful to pray for him, aloud, as we kneel together, and then to encourage him to pour out his heart to the Lord aloud as well, although he will not be used to it. This enables him both to clarify and verbalize his feelings and also to get used to verbal prayer in his own words from the very outset of his spiritual pilgrimage. However short and stumbling his prayer, he, like the publican in the Gospels, can go to his house justified, for he has cried to and been heard by the Supreme Mercy. He is going to need a lot of help, not least from the person who helped him to faith, but for the moment it will suffice that he has begun.

Chapter 4

The extent of their after-care

If you look at the account of the day of Pentecost, you cannot help being struck by the impact made by the Holy Spirit, by the transformation of the apostles and by the number of those who responded. But equally significant is the immediate after-care given to the new converts by the original disciples. They were at once baptized, and then continued in the apostles' doctrine and fellowship, the breaking of the bread and the prayers (Acts 2:42).

After-care is as vital as birth. If not cared for, the new babe in Christ will starve. And a great deal of contemporary evangelism is pathetically weak in following up and helping on those who have professed the faith.

Let us look at some of the elements in the early church's programme of after-care.

They baptized new believers

There can be no doubt that in the first days of the church baptism was administered as soon as possible after profession of faith. Quite apart from the day of Pentecost, the case of the Philippian jailer and the Ethiopian eunuch give a good guide to early practice in this matter. Commitment to Christ, baptism in water, and reception of the Holy Spirit were three sides of the same thing, Christian initiation. In Galatians, for instance, we see that justification by faith or becoming 'Abraham's offspring' comes about through reception of the Spirit, or being baptized into Christ, or believing in Christ (3:2, 14, 29, 26). Ideally, they belonged together. In practice, however, sometimes one element would come first, sometimes another: such is still the case.

Two second-century developments can be traced back, at least in outline, to the early days of the church. First, there was a growing tendency to postpone baptism, preface it by a period of instruction, and perform it, along with first communion, at the highly significant season of Good Friday and Easter. Scholars have seen many signs in the New Testament itself of a basic catechism leading up to baptism, and many people think that 1 Peter was written as a homily for a baptism occasion.

Infant baptism?

Second was the practice of baptizing infants when born into a believing family. This is a divisive subject nowadays, and was at the end of the second century when we find Tertullian discussing it in his *Treatise on Baptism*. He was advocating delay in baptism when only one parent was a believer: it is clear that he wrote against a background where the baptism of infants was common. How could this be justified when originally baptism was the mark of the new birth, and appropriate only for believers?

Well, I doubt if baptism was ever quite as clear-cut as that. We read in the New Testament of whole households being baptized, and an ancient household comprised not only the children but the slaves, all of whom were committed by the action of the head of the house (1 Cor. 1:16; Acts 16:33, *etc.*) You see, baptism was not exclusively the act of man, representing his faith: it was also the act of God, representing his grace. And that free grace of God sent Jesus to the cross to die for us and rise again whether or not we ever respond. It is that once-for-allness of Jesus, his sacrifice and triumph, which is marked upon us in baptism. It should ideally be matched by our total and immediate response. But that sometimes comes

82

later—and sometimes does not come at all. Even if it never follows, that cannot destroy the initiative of God, who gave himself for us once in history: that holds good whether or not we respond—though of course we cannot make any use of his gift unless we receive it in adoring gratitude. By far the largest part of the Christian church has believed it right to baptize not only believers but their children. The Baptist view regards baptism as appropriate only for those who have already responded in faith to God's gracious initiative. Christians will continue to have differing views on this matter since no clear biblical teaching settles it one way or the other. And as far as the nurture of new believers is concerned, you will find that some of your converts have already been baptized (generally in infancy) while others have not.

Rebaptism?

I believe that those who have already been baptized should not be rebaptized. It makes no more sense to be baptized again than to be justified again or to enter the Lord's family again. Baptism emphasizes the once-for-allness of our incorporation into Christ, and by its nature cannot be repeated: communion is frequently repeated and stresses the ongoing side of the Christian life. You will only confuse the issue if you rebaptize, however strong the inducement to do so. And the inducement is strong, especially among young men and women who want to seal their faith in this public sacrament of commitment and regard their baptism in infancy as useless. Of course it was useless, like an uncashed cheque, until they claimed it. Now they have done the claiming, now the inward mixture matches the label on the bottle, they do not need to get a fresh label all over again. But they do need to have an opportunity of publicly confessing their faith. This is clearly enjoined upon them in Scripture, and a chance should be given them to do it early on in their Christian lives (Rom. 10.9–11). This is where the practice of confirmation is especially important for paedo-baptists (for Baptists the confessional element is central to their baptism). It enables someone personally to reiterate and underline the promises made on his behalf in baptism as a child. It also gives

83

him that opportunity of public confession which is his duty and right. And as he confirms his side of the convenant, the bishop's hands on his head represent the loving hands of the Father assuring him of acceptance and protection, and commissioning him for service. At confirmation in our church in Oxford the great majority are adults, and none are presented without making a clear profession of faith before the congregation in their own words. It is also a help to have an opportunity for public confession for those who turn to Christ after they have already been baptized and confirmed. We ask the bishop at the confirmation to have special prayer with each of these people as they set out to 'possess their possessions'.

Immediate baptism?

Those who have not already been baptized need to express their faith in Christ publicly in this sacrament of initiation. There are two views on when this should be. Some believe that it should be as early as possible, and that the new believer should then undergo careful training for full church membership or confirmation. Others think it is better to delay baptism until after a good time of preparation and teaching, and let it be combined with whatever other initiation into full church membership the church in question requires. For the record, we tend to choose the former option, but it could be argued either way.

They gave regular instruction

'They continued in the apostles' teaching,' so Acts tells us of the early converts. What would that involve? Well, it would certainly involve three areas.

The Scriptures

First, there was Scripture. It was only the Old Testament, of course, in the Greek Septuagint translation, but it certainly became the Bible of the early Christians. You find literally hundreds of quotations from it in the New Testament letters, and it is plain that the converts had got to know it well. Like

Jesus, and indeed all of Judaism except the Sadducees, the early Christian believed that all scripture was God-given and profitable (2 Tim. 3:16). Behind its human authors stood God's Holy Spirit which inspired it (2 Pet. 1:19–21; 1 Pet. 1:10–12). So they learnt to use it with reverence. They knew that God who had spoken partially through the Old Testament spoke fully and finally in Jesus, and so they searched the Old Testament scriptures for light upon Jesus, in prediction, allegory or type. So fundamental was this reference to Scripture that when Paul leaves the Ephesian elders he commends them to God (natural enough in any parting) but also to his gracious word which is able to build them up and show them more and more of their inheritance as Christians.

This remains one of the most fundamental essentials for new Christians. They need to be helped to read the Bible. They may have read it before in school. They may have admired it as literature. But they need to see it as the milk without which babies die (1 Pet. 2:2), the strong meat for mature believers (Heb. 5:12–14), the light they need to be shed on their path (Ps. 119:105), the hammer that may from time to time be needed to shatter the rock of self-will in their lives (Je. 23:29). Scripture is vital to growth, and they need to discover this.

The most obvious ways are these. Someone needs to see that they have a readable Bible, preferably in some modern translation. It is a good idea to give them one of the many Bible reading aids, such as Scripture Union notes, International Bible Reading Association notes, *Every Day with Jesus, Search the Scriptures, Food for Life* or *The Soldier's Armoury*. It is an even better idea for you to read with them on the first occasion, showing them how to see what the passage meant originally and then applying that to their own situation; leading them to a promise, a command, or a warning that is relevant to their situation; looking for a prayer to use, or a key thought to commit to memory for the day. You will want them to jot down what they have learnt from the passage, maybe, or what action it prompts. In this way you will expose them to the thrill of Scripture as a living, talking book. I find it a good thing to turn to prayer after a session of reading like that. I suggest that we each take a verse, or part of a verse, that has helped us and either thank God for it or ask that it may be true of us—a mere one-sentence prayer. In this way the new believer is encouraged to launch out on the uncharted waters of prayer. This is where he begins—with the Bible read devotionally and prayer springing from it. It is a combination essential to growth.

The life and teaching of Jesus

In addition to the scriptures of the Old Testament the early converts were certainly taught about the person and teaching of Jesus, and the Holy Spirit who had come from him into their midst. It is a commonplace among those who study the New Testament in depth that the material we find in the Gospels had gone through many hands before it was first written down. There was an early collection of the sayings of Jesus, lost now as an independent document, but embodied in the parallel teaching material we find in Matthew and Luke. Such a document would in any case have been necessary. New converts would want to know what their Master taught. There was equal interest in what he did, particularly his healings and exorcisms (which might often be continued among them by the Spirit) and the events leading up to his death. You find a short edition of this in Acts 10:38–43, and more extended treatment in the Gospel of Mark and indeed the other Gospels as well. And the extent to which new believers were grounded in the teaching about Jesus, his Spirit, his church, his future, is abundantly plain from the Letters. I am constantly staggered, as I wrestle with them, to recall that these letters were originally sent to people of little education, many of whom were slaves! How they must have bent their minds to understand the revelation made to them in Christ.

In any modern church that is fit to be entrusted with new believers there must be a teaching programme to enable them to 'know whom they have believed' and to 'grow in grace and the knowledge of their Lord and Saviour Jesus Christ'. In our own church we put new Christians into 'beginners' groups', which have a structured content of teaching over an eight-week period, along with the type of devotional Bible study and prayer described above. Subjects such as Christian assurance, the Bible, prayer, the church, the person and death of Christ, the resurrection, the Holy Spirit, together with Christian service—these are some of the themes dealt with. There is a hand-out of duplicated material for people to use when they get home. And after this eight-week course members are fed into other teaching organizations which help them towards Christian maturity.

An early Christian catechism

Recent study of the New Testament has suggested that there may well have been a third strand of teaching which we can trace back to the first days of the church. Comparison of some of the Letters and the material they have in common suggests that there was a catechetical framework in frequent use among Christian leaders in those days. Romans 6:17 thanks God that they have obeyed the 'form' or 'mould' of teaching to which they have been committed, and the same idea is present in the letters to the Thessalonians and to Timothy and Titus. What did this ethical teaching consist of?

In Colossians there is the sequence 'Put off the old nature' (3:9), 'Put on the new nature' (3:10), 'Submit' (3:18), 'Watch and pray' (4:2), 'Stand' (4:12). This may look like an arbitrary selection until you see a similar pattern elsewhere. Ephesians has the same. 'Put off' (4:22), 'Put on' (4:24), 'Submit' (5:22), 'Stand' (6:11), 'Watch and pray' (6:18). 1 Peter begins with a strong emphasis on the new birth (1:23), and follows it with 'Put off' (2:1), 'Worship' (2:4–9), 'Submit' (2:13—and he spells it out until 5:9 as it applies to husbands, wives, citizens, and leaders), 'Watch and pray' (4:7), 'Resist' (5:8–9). James also starts with the new birth (1:18), and follows it with 'Put off' (1:21), 'Be subject' (4:7), 'Resist the devil' (4:7), and 'Pray' (5:16). Almost all the passages have strong references to love for the brethren, and this is spelt out in detail in Ephesians, Colossians and James. While we cannot be too sure about the details of this 'catechism', it is certainly significant that broadly the same pattern recurs in three such different writers as Paul,

Peter and James, and we are probably right to see here the skeleton of a teaching course either leading up to baptism or on from baptism in the earliest church. It could make a marvellous course today.

First, a session on the new birth, and the radical transformation it will bring with it. The convert needs to be sure about it: otherwise he will build on a shaky foundation.

Secondly, an examination of some of the things belonging to the old life which need to be laid aside, and indeed can be, like last year's leaves still clinging to a tree, when the new sap rises.

Thirdly, a lesson on the image of God in which man was made; lost through man's disobedience in the fall; fully restored in the person of Jesus; and gradually imparted to the believer by the Spirit as he changes us into the likeness of our Lord. This new life has to be put on, deliberately and in faith, day by day—like a fresh outfit of clothes.

Fourthly, Christians are not called to boss others around, but to live their lives in submission to their Lord and to one another. The husband must as much submit to his wife in loving care and protection as she must submit to him as the leader in the family. And the same applies in our relations with the state and with one another. Jesus lived the life of the Servant, and we must follow him, unpalatable as it may sound. It is an astonishing tribute to the Spirit of Jesus in Peter that he who once had been so proud and independent should make mutual submission, following the example of Jesus, such a major plank in his first Letter.

Fifthly, the new believer needs to be taught to 'stand' or 'withstand' the evil one. Temptation will increase: he has made a great enemy as well as a great Friend. He needs to learn total opposition to every manifestation of the enemy, and an implicit trust in the mighty power of Jesus.

Sixthly, he needs to watch and pray. It is interesting that the two should come together. But unless he watches he will not pray: the prayer time will get squeezed out. And unless he watches in another sense, he will not go on praying. For he will not notice answers to prayer and will become discouraged. Watch and pray.

In addition the area of love and worship seem to have been covered by the early Christians. What a course for new believers that would make!

They provided fellowship

The earliest believers 'continued in the apostles' fellowship', we are told. The warmth of that fellowship is abundantly plain from the pages of the New Testament.

Personal attention

The first requirement in Christian fellowship is normally some other individual who has been a Christian for some while and is able and willing to give time and deep interest to the new brother or sister in Christ. Post-natal neglect is a common cause of death among Christians, for although many Christians have an interest in evangelism, few take the time and trouble to build their converts up in the faith. Yet where would Saul have been after his Damascus Road experience without Ananias to help him in the initial stages, or without Barnabas, the great encourager, to come alongside him and introduce him to the Christians in Jerusalem? We all need an Ananias or a Barnabas.

I recall how I used to make a list of my early problems and difficulties in Christian discipleship and then take them along once a fortnight or so to Richard Gorrie, who was a few years older than I and a more mature Christian. I shall never cease to be grateful for the help he gave me in those early days; for the encouragement it was to meet him and learn from him when all around me there were those who did not share my faith or know my Lord, and also for the example that he unwittingly afforded me of the wise Christian pastor at work. For this is just what he was. As Paul wrote years later, perhaps thinking back to his own early days, 'Though you have countless guides in Christ, you do not have many fathers. For I became your father in Christ through the gospel' (1 Cor. 4:15). We have seen Paul's concern for one of his converts, in his little letter to Philemon. Philemon was a Christian landowner whose slave,

89

Onesimus, had run away and landed up in the same jail as Paul. He had been converted by the apostle, and had decided that he must, in conscience, return to Philemon, but was fearing his reception, so Paul wrote a covering letter for him. 'I appeal to you for my child, Onesimus, whose father I have become in my imprisonment ... I am sending him back to you, sending my very heart' (verses 10, 12). There was the pastor who really cared and took trouble over his convert. This is the sort of thing Paul must have had in mind when he wrote of his own relations with the very new Thessalonian church. 'We were gentle among you, like a nurse taking care of her children' (1 Thes. 2:7). Sometimes the gentleness of the nurse needs to be supplemented with the wise direction of the father, so Paul continues in the same context, 'You know how, like a father with his children, we exhorted each one of you and encouraged you and charged you to lead a life worthy of God who calls you into his own kingdom and glory' (2:11f.). A new Christian needs help and encouragement like that. It is wise to assign each new believer to someone older in the faith who will nurse him and father him until he grows roots of his own. People are most vulnerable in the early days of discipleship, and they need this personal opportunity to share difficulties and doubts. I find that a weekly time embodying some social activity and a meal, the opportunity to talk over problems and a short time of reading the Bible together and praying, is an invaluable way of building a new disciple into the body.

Church worship

For the body of Christ is what he has joined. The images of Christians in the New Testament are almost all plural: he is a sheep in the flock, a soldier in the army, a limb in the body, a stone in the building and so forth. Christianity is a very corporate affair. We are not meant to be independent nor to go it alone. We do not travel from the alone to the Alone: we travel to the Trinity in fellowship. The church, then, is an essential part of God's purposes. It is the first instalment of the kingdom of God, and within it the law of the kingdom, the law of love and mutual service, runs large. All Christians need the

90

church, just as the church needs all Christians. Public worship and smaller, more informal expressions of Christian fellowship are alike essential to growth. We see the early believers worshipping not only in temple and synagogue, but also informally from house to house. Happy the church that embraces both modes of worship.

We need the big gathering of Christians in glad and wholehearted worship. We need to extol the praises of our Redeemer. We need to pray to him together concerning the great needs of his people and his world. We need to be exposed to a balanced reading of the Scriptures and preaching of the word. We need to come and confess how far short we fall as outriders of God's kingdom and how warped an idea we often convey of who he is and what he is about in the world. Public worship is a must. This is how the New Testament puts it: 'Let us hold fast the confession of our hope without wavering, for he who promised is faithful; and let us consider how to stir up one another to love and good works, not neglecting to meet together, as is the habit of some, but encouraging one another, and all the more as you see the Day drawing near' (Heb. 10:23ff.). We need the strength, the encouragement, the stimulus, the teaching and the prayer of corporate worship. But it cannot stop there.

Alas, in many churches it does stop there. Nothing happens from one week's end to another so far as Christian fellowship is concerned. And often there is very little togetherness, very little opportunity to share personal concerns in the worship service itself. Both of these weaknesses need to be rectified if we want to see vital worship among the Christian family and real growth as a family of God. If the church congregation is small (up to 200 or so) it is very possible to incorporate some time of sharing news and concerns within the period of worship itself. In an Anglican church this can often be during the extended Peace which comes in the middle of a Holy Communion service. But it could equally well come at the end, or when prayer requests are asked for before the intercession. If people feel they matter, then they gain that vital sense of belonging which is essential for the body of Christ to display. If they feel they are merely 'pew fodder', before long they will either shrivel up or drift away. God's Frozen People simply have to escape from the bonds of their many conservatisms and thaw out, at least to the extent of sharing with fellow Christians in church some of the burdens on their hearts or the joys and answers to prayer they are experiencing. And anything that can help that thawing process is to be encouraged: a variety of people reading the lessons, leading the prayers, assisting in various ways, leading in song, with instrument or with dance, coffee or lunch after the service and so on. For Christian worship is not intended to be the predictable uniformity of the graveyard but an expression of the vibrant life of the people of God.

Informal fellowship

But the people of God exist throughout the week, too! There needs to be provision for informal fellowship among believers, particularly those who are single and do not enjoy the partnership of a Christian home. Many churches find that an informal meeting for worship, teaching, prayer and sheer enjoyment of our liberation in Christ is a marvellous mid-week encouragement and strength. I have known new believers come to our mid-week fellowship a day or two after their conversion, and bear testimony to the new hope that is within them. Three things then happen. The meeting is thrilled; the new believer is strengthened by having spoken up for his Lord: and he finds he really fits in this company of God's people— although he has never been to anything like it before in his life! The time afterwards over coffee is a marvellous opportunity to mingle, to share interests and news, and to minister to one another appropriately: often you see couples and threesomes in a corner finding solace and strength in praying together over some problem that is troubling one of them. Thus the fellowship grows.

A development of the mid-week meeting is the growth of area fellowship groups. There is nothing very original in this. It is merely the gathering together of members of that church who happen to live in the same part of town. They get together over a meal, learn to love and value one another, and meet regularly to study, to support one another, and to see what they can do in service to the neighbourhood. These groups are particularly essential in a large congregation or Christian Union. Otherwise it is fatally easy to be carried along by the group spirituality of the large body and never have a chance to contribute or to ask for help with needs.

If personal caring, membership of a group, and exposure to regular worship in church is all part of the fare on which the new believer is fed, there is every chance that he will 'grow in grace and in the knowledge of our Lord and Saviour Jesus Christ' (2 Pet. 3:18).

Visits and letters

But there were two subsidiary ways in which new Christians were nourished in the earliest days, ways in which we sometimes miss out. In the first place, the apostles and other leading Christians made a lot of visits to see how their converts were getting on, and to encourage them in the faith. Paul's words to Barnabas in Acts 15:36 are typical of the attitude that prevailed in those days. 'Come, let us return and visit the brethren in every city where we proclaimed the word of the Lord, and see how they are.' The more we can visit those whom we have helped to faith, the better. For there is that unique link between those who are parents and children in Christ through the gospel. It is a link to be exploited.

The other way is equally obvious: to use a letter instead of a visit. The apostles did. But what letters! I think the art of letter writing is past, in this age of breathless haste and instant everything. Hardly anybody sits down nowadays to write from the heart about the Lord to other Christians. There is no doubt that we impoverish ourselves by neglecting the letter. Think of the blessing to millions that the correspondence of Peter and Paul, James and John has been. Think of what the world owes to the letters of a Newton or a Rutherford. It is interesting to see that even a man as busy and famous as C. S. Lewis made time to correspond regularly with an American lady on spiritual things, a correspondence which has happily been

93

made available after his death. Letters to young Christians make an enormous lot of difference. A remarkable clergyman, the Rev. E. J. H. Nash, used to write to me (and to hundreds of others) regularly two or three times a term when I was a schoolboy, battling with the early stages of discipleship. He often had very little to say, but he said it with humour and charm. And he loved to add a verse from the Bible and a word of comment which seemed time and again to meet the exact need I was experiencing. Those letters meant more in my growth as a Christian than ever I realized at the time. I thank God for them.

They exercised oversight

This comes to us as some surprise. In the first place, hardly any churches outside the Roman Catholic have known what oversight and discipline are in the centuries since the Reformation. Second, democracy has become so widely accepted as a model, indeed the model, not only in the body politic but in home and business and industry and the church as well, that we tend to look askance at those areas of the Bible which point to another pattern. And unquestionably they do point to a quite different model.

Requirements for leadership

In Scripture, the people of God are a theocracy. They are not ruled by one person, or by a few, or by themselves, but by God. He exercises his leadership through a variety of means, none of which is regulative. So we find prophets, kings, judges, elders, apostles, teachers, jostling alongside the direct inter-vention of God's Holy Spirit in the leadership of his people. And in the New Testament we find a variety of ecclesial patterns: congregationalism, presbyterianism, episcopacy, Catholicism, all claim to find models in the New Testament which point to their own form of church government. I am not concerned to evaluate these varied patterns: merely to point out that they exist. What concerns me at this point is the fact that new Christians were assigned to those who were over

94

them in the Lord (1 Thes. 5:12). There were under-shepherds in the Lord's flock, and these had charge of the flock and represented the Lord himself in their care of it (Acts 20:28).

It is clear from two lists of qualities contained in the Epistles what the qualities desirable in such people were: they should not be recent converts, or they might get conceited; they were to have admirable personal qualities and family lives; they were to be well thought-of by the congregation and by outsiders; and they were to have a gift of teaching (Tit. 1:5–9; 1 Tim. 3:1–7). The purpose of these 'elders', 'presbyters' or 'shepherds', as they seem to have been called, was clear. It was to build up the Christians for their work of service to God (Eph. 4:12). In particular they were called to preach, teach, probably to lead in worship (though the New Testament nowhere indicates this) and to care for people. This caring included practical offers of help to brethren in need (Rom. 16:1–2), giving warning and building up (Acts 20:28–32), affording hospitality (3 John 6–7) and living an exemplary Christian life which other believers could profitably follow (Phil. 4:9). It was when leadership was of this quality that the New Testament writers could exhort believers to obey it out of love for Christ. This note of obedience comes out again and again in Paul's dealings with the recalcitrant Corinthian church, and in 1 Thessalonians 5:12ff., 2 Thessalonians 3:10–15 and elsewhere.

Dangers of leadership

In recent years one of the fastest-growing Christian move-ments has been the network of house churches throughout the world. These are independent Christian organizations owing no allegiance to any main-line church, and linked only very informally to any body outside their own local house church. Part of the strength of this movement is the practical caring which members show for one another, not only in the ordinary affairs of life but in spiritual growth and development. But so strong has been this emphasis on individual caring and what is called 'delegated authority' (held in a chain going up through the pastor to the Lord) that something dangerously akin to authoritarianism can—and sometimes does—ensue. When you must implicitly obey your 'cover', as the one above you in the chain is called, and obey him as you would obey the Lord, then something is seriously amiss. Part of the value of being a body, part of the value of a shared eldership (as you always find in the New Testament) is to preserve Christians from the vagaries of one individual leader. We need variety in those over us in the Lord: we also need them to exercise their lead with a gentle sensitivity which will allow us to grow up as the Lord designed us to be, rather than as pale copies of the one who is over us in the Lord. The Corinthian correspondence is full of warnings against those who erected a Paul, an Apollos, a Peter into infallible guides. We are not to overvalue spiritual leaders, but neither are we to despise them. Peter in his first Letter has an invaluable chapter on the matter. In chapter 5 he sets himself alongside the elders to whom he writes, not as a management figure but as a 'fellow elder'. Like them, he has one eye upon the cross of Christ and one eye upon the glory to be revealed. And with a backward gaze at what it cost Christ to purchase the flock, and a forward glance to what he has in store for the flock, Peter urges the 'under-shepherds' to feed the flock with tenderness and individual care, just as Jesus had fed Peter. That flock is their responsibility. They are to tend it not because they have to, but because they want to. They are to tend it not for what they can get out of it, but for what they can put into it. They are to tend it not as bosses but as examples. And he holds up for their emulation the towel of the servant, in the rare word he uses in verse 5 for 'clothe yourselves'. It is the word used of Jesus at the Last Supper when he 'girded himself' with a towel and washed his disciples' feet. That is the quality of leadership which merits following.

Laying foundations

One particular area where the new convert will value this lead, whether exercised by the person who led him to the faith or somebody else, is in the whole matter of reorienting his life as a Christian. There will be problems of belief, of behaviour, of relationships and so on, to be talked over and wisely handled. But perhaps the most important initial matter will be the question of whether the believer can know where he stands. Can he be confident that this act of commitment was not merely a flash in the pan, a burst of emotion? Can he be sure that the Lord has received him? Or is he condemned to perpetual insecurity on this crucial issue?

Crucial it is, though frequently brushed under the carpet. Many people today would think it entirely improper, indeed rather indecent, to be confident that you are a Christian, that you are forgiven, that you are a member of the body of Christ and on the road for heaven. Disgusting! Arrogant in the extreme! But is it?

It seems to me that there are at least three good reasons why we can be confident on this matter, apart from the obvious one that nobody can build any house, let alone the house of Christian discipleship, on an insecure foundation. The first reason is that Jesus Christ did so assure people. He told the dying thief that he would that day be with him in Paradise. He told his disciples that they would reign with him in heaven. He told us that he would never cast out anyone who came to him (John 6:37) and that if we received his Spirit into our lives we would be born again into his family (John 3:3). He told us that he came to seek and to save the lost, and expected people like Zacchaeus to know that they had in fact been reached by his saving love (Luke 19:9–10). In short, if you believe Jesus Christ, you can scarcely doubt the propriety of knowing you are forgiven.

The second reason is very similar. The New Testament writers were in no doubt about their own salvation and that of the people to whom they wrote. Just glance, for instance, through Ephesians 1. 'God has blessed us in Christ with every spiritual blessing . . . He chose us in him before the foundation of the world . . . he destined us in love to be his sons . . . in him we have redemption through his blood, the forgiveness of our trespasses' and so on. They are in no doubt about it, and the inference is that neither should we be.

The third reason is this: we are justified freely by God's

97

grace, not by our own fancied achievements. Now, if my presence in God's heaven were due to my own good deeds, I must for ever be unsure if my deeds were good enough. But if I depend on the finished work of Christ on the cross for my forgiveness, then that is a very different matter. There is no question of arrogance, now. It is a matter of believing that when God gives me the gift of forgiveness, eternal life and membership of his family then he intends me to know that I have got it—and not to insult him by continuing to doubt.

A humble, grateful, adoring assurance that I do in fact belong is, then, my birthright as a Christian. Although, mercifully, it is the task of the Holy Spirit himself to make believers know that they are in the family of God (Rom. 8:15–17), he often works through some human agent to help us see it.

The 'under-shepherd', then, has the initial task of showing the new convert that his standing in Christ is not dependent on his own fluctuating feelings, but on the promises of God and on the finished work of Jesus Christ. Promises such as John 6:37, John 1:12, Revelation 3:20, Hebrews 13:5, 1 John 1:8–9 and 5:9–12 should be carefully explained to the young believer, until he sees that God means us to take him at his word, and that even when we let him down and fall into sin he does not cast us out of his family: the blood of Jesus Christ, his Son, goes on cleansing us from all sin. But in addition to the word of God the Father and the work of God the Son—that finished work of Calvary which can never be repeated nor augmented—there is the witness of the Spirit which the new believer needs to understand. We know we are in God's family, because of 'the Spirit which he has given us' (1 John 3:24).

That Spirit makes himself known in a variety of ways. I have spelled them out in a book designed for new Christians, called *New Life, New Lifestyle*. But the essence of them, as John shows us in his first Letter, is as follows. The Holy Spirit assures us of his presence by giving us a whole range of new experience. He gives us a new desire to obey God (2:3), a new hatred of the old paths of sin (3:9), a new joy in the company of Jesus and his followers (1:3f.), a new discovery that prayer is real (5:14f.), a new love for brother Christians (3:14), a new outgoing care towards anybody in need (3:17f.), and a new experience of the inner power of the Spirit to overcome in the battle with temptation (4:4; 5:4). These are some of the indicators, along with the promises of God and the objective facts of Calvary and the resurrection, which assure the new Christian that he has indeed begun. The marks of new life do not all come at once. They do not come in any particular order. But come they do, as the Holy Spirit is given free rein in the life. And gradually 1 John 5:13 becomes true: 'I write to you who believe in the name of the Son of God, that you may know that you have eternal life.' And it is to this confidence that the Christian leader will seek to bring his friend. Once that foundation is firmly laid, the way of growth is open. But the leader does not complete his job until he can produce the convert mature in Christ, and able to win others also. That, and nothing less, is the goal of Christian pastoral care.

They engaged in prayer

The early converts continued in the apostles' 'prayers', or 'prayer times' as Acts 2:42 could equally well be translated. Many of them on that day of Pentecost were already used to personal and liturgical prayer. They were either Jews or proselytes, that is to say hangers-on at the synagogue. But now they found prayer a totally different thing. It was prayer 'through Jesus Christ', or 'in his name'. God was known for the first time as 'Abba', 'dear Father', with an intimacy unheard of in Judaism or any other religion. Jesus was the way to God, and to ask through him the sort of prayers to which he could have been expected to put his name meant an unprecedented assurance that those prayers would be heard and answered as the heavenly Father thought best. 'Ask, and you shall receive', Jesus had said. These people were beginning to do just that.

Personal prayer

There seem to have been three areas in which their prayers were revolutionized. The first was in the private sphere. They

99

began to be conscious of the Holy Spirit helping them in their natural prayerlessness, and making them able to address the Father with their needs. The barrier of separation between them and God had been broken down, and prayer began to be a reality and a joy. When Saul of Tarsus was converted, the only proof of the genuineness of that conversion vouchsafed to Ananias, who was sent by God to follow him up, was this: 'Behold, he is praying' (Acts 9:11). Now at last he was getting through to God. He was in touch. Often I have had a new believer make the same point to me. 'Now I feel I am not just praying to the ceiling. I am getting through.' That was, after all, one of the great objectives in the atonement. He 'died for us so that whether we wake or sleep we might live with him' (1 Thes. 5:10).

Public prayer

The second area was public prayer. These men and women who had found in Jesus their Messiah continued worshipping in the temple and synagogue, but there was a new spring in their step. You can practically hear the joy and confidence exuding from them in the record of the Acts. 'And day by day, attending the temple together and breaking bread in their homes, they partook of food with glad and generous hearts, praising God . . .', they 'were continually in the temple blessing God . . .' (Acts 2:46f.; Lk. 24:52). We have another glimpse of them when the lame man had been healed at the Beautiful Gate of the temple. 'And leaping up he stood and walked and entered the temple with them, walking and leaping and praising God.' This led to impromptu preaching in the temple, and the excitement is clear for all to see even in the account of the displeasure of the Sadducees at this disturbance of the normal ritual. 'The Sadducees came upon them, annoyed because they were teaching the people and proclaiming in Jesus the resurrection from the dead. And they arrested them . . .' (4:2f.).

Temple worship then would have many of the overtones of cathedral worship now. Sonorous, beautiful, predictable, perfectly rendered, but perhaps a little lacking in life. It is noteworthy that the early converts did not write it off as hopelessly unspiritual and dull. They went to it with radiant joy, and that joy became infectious and eventually seems to have caused a split. The new life could not be contained in the old forms, and the new forms of the Christian church had to be discovered instead. Now the church itself is old and set in its ways, but it is still the duty of those newly filled with the wine of the Spirit to throw their weight in with the public worship in their area, even though it may call for a lot of patience on both sides. In extreme cases they may get thrown out, but on the whole most churches will be glad to see an incursion of new life. The welding together of old and new calls for much wisdom, but it can be done. If the church is a Free Church there should in principle be some hope of free participation for new believers in open prayer and testimony. If you belong to a church which has a formal liturgy the chances for this may be fewer, but the liturgy itself has stood the test of time and if you enter into the spirit of it it is possible to be lifted up to heaven in worship and adoration: and the ancient time-honoured words can be a help rather than a hindrance. Like many things, however, it is an acquired taste, and requires practice!

Public worship generally gives plenty of opportunity for praise, and if you have recently come to Christ praise will be a very important part of your spiritual agenda. You will quickly discover that 'God inhabits the praises of Israel'—that is to say, he is especially present when his people begin to praise him. We praise him for what he is, Creator, Redeemer, Indweller, eternal Lover, source of life and joy and peace. And these factors remain constant whether or not we have anything particular to thank him for at present for what he is doing in our lives. Praise is a vital part of the Christian life. It opens us up to God's blessings and makes us sensitive to his presence in a way little else does. And praise is much easier in company with other Christians than on one's own. So the sooner the new believer can get used to going to church to praise God from the bottom of his heart in the psalms and hymns and spiritual songs provided, the better for his spiritual health. And the corporate prayer, especially for needs much wider

101

than he would pray for on his own, and in a building that has been hallowed by generations of believers praying to their Father, has a value all its own.

Group prayer

A third dimension of prayer makes its appearance in the pages of the Acts. This is prayer in a group. There is an excellent example in Acts 4 when the two apostles, Peter and John, after their release from prison join the others in a meeting not for protest but for prayer. We are given a glimpse of the inside of an early prayer meeting in the verses that follow. We sense their unity—'they lifted their voices together to God' (verse 24). They relied entirely on the sovereignty of God and saw prayer as a way to discover his will rather than an attempt to change it (25ff.). They made good use of the psalms in their prayers (26f.), and they simply spread out their needs before the Lord without suggesting what he should do about it. But they did ask for courage to witness boldly for their Lord and for his power to be present among them (29f.). The outcome of that prayer is noteworthy, too. 'When they had prayed, the place in which they were gathered together was shaken; and they were all filled with the Holy Spirit and spoke the word of God with boldness.' There are a good many other examples of such informal prayer in small groups throughout the New Testament. A notable one was when Peter was in prison under Herod Agrippa. 'Peter was kept in prison; but earnest prayer for him was made to God by the church' (Acts 12:5). Prayer was made. It was united prayer. It was earnest prayer. It was God-directed prayer. It was specific prayer. But even so, when the answer to their prayers walked in the door, nobody believed it (14ff.). A very human touch! I am touched, too, by the spontaneity of a beach-side prayer meeting, recorded in Acts 20:36ff. The Ephesian elders are persuaded that they will never see their friend and mentor Paul again. 'And when he had spoken thus, he knelt down and prayed with them all. And they all wept and embraced Paul and kissed him, sorrowing most of all because of the word he had spoken, that they should see his face no more. And they brought him to the ship.'

It is clear, then, that Christians in the early days prayed privately, in worship services and also in small groups as they met in each other's houses, or even in the open air. It is the natural thing for Christians to do when they are together: after all, they are children of the same heavenly Father. And the sooner a new believer learns to feel at home in all three modes of prayer, the richer his spiritual experience will be. In this area, as in so many others, he is going to need the help and support and instruction of those who have been Christians rather longer.

They celebrated the Holy Communion

The Holy Communion figured a great deal more prominently in the worship of the early Christians than it does in most Protestant denominations these days. Unlike the Passover from which it sprang, it was observed not annually but often: probably once a week on the day of the resurrection, the 'Lord's day' as Christians speedily began to call it (Rev. 1:10). The communion was the sacrament of Christian growth just as baptism was of Christian birth.

We can get some idea of those early communions from three places in the New Testament. In Acts 2:42, 46 we read that the converts continued in the 'breaking of bread', and that this took place 'in their homes'. One envisages a group of Christians eating a meal together and ending by breaking bread as Jesus had taught them, in thankful remembrance of his self-giving for them on Calvary. This generally took place at night, we may be sure. For then the work of the day was over and there was plenty of time

The second little cameo of a communion service comes from Acts 20, where Paul is the honoured guest as believers meet to break bread at Troas on the first day of the week. This was the famous occasion when Paul preached so long that Eutychus fell asleep and dropped out of the window. But the young man was healed, and the service went on until daybreak. The communion in those days would be much more of a meal than it is today, and an opportunity for much informal worship and fellowship. The meal time was called an *agapē*, a love-feast, and in later times it fell into disuse because it was much abused. It would seem from Jude 12 that immorality sometimes broke out in these intimate gatherings for worship, and 1 Corinthians 11, our third main passage on the eucharist, makes it clear that some Christians were very thoughtless.

The Christian passover

The rich came early at Corinth and ate all the meal, while the slaves who had to work late arrived half way through to find that there was nothing left. Some love-feast! So Paul rebukes them sharply, and reminds them of the way in which they should approach this holy meal. It is the Christian passover (1 Cor. 5:7), and like the passover it has three tenses. As the passover enshrined a *backward* look to the blood of the lamb which secured release for the captives in Egypt (Ex. 12), so the communion looks back to the blood of Jesus which secured release for sin's captives at Calvary (1 Cor. 11:25). Both meals had an *upward* look to the Lord who feeds and sustains his people: for the Israelite the passover was food for the tough journey ahead; and the Christian in the eucharist is nourished with the very body and blood of Christ (1 Cor. 10:16). The passover had a third aspect, as it looked *forward* to the land of promise. So has the Christian passover, 'for as often as you eat this bread and drink this cup, you proclaim the Lord's death until he comes' (11:26). The Holy Communion anticipates the consummation of all history, and it is that aspect of it which is dominant in Luke's account (Lk. 22:14–30). Such being the dynamic nature of the communion meal, as dynamic and all-embracing as the salvation of which it is the sacrament, it is hardly surprising that Paul urges the Corinthians to come with self-examination to this holy supper (1 Cor. 11:28). The person who comes carelessly is guilty of profaning and insulting the body and blood of the Lord (27). Indeed, illness and even death can be traced to this profanation (30f.), so it is vital that Christians come together in unity, with humility and mutual consideration. They must eat sparingly and do nothing to hurt any other member of the Lord's body. Then the Lord's supper would indeed be a foretaste of heaven. It would be a joyful, triumphant remembrance of the cross and resurrection, as together in unity and love they feed on the body and blood of the Lord.

It will take the new believer many years to understand the depths of the Holy Communion. He will never fully plumb them. But he can start to be fed by this holy meal as soon as he is baptized into Christ (although many churches expect further instruction and initiation before admitting converts to full communicating membership).

Communion – the main service?

Historically it is true to say that the Catholics have stressed the sacrament and the Protestants the word as the means of grace for Christian growth. Manifestly both views are one-sided. Why should we limp along on one leg when the good Lord has given us two? The Lord Jesus in his wisdom has left us a mystery, the mystery of his own person and sacrifice, at the very heart of our worship; and the deeper we get into it the deeper we shall get into him. Many Protestant churches are discovering the centrality of the Holy Communion, which the Roman Catholics and the Christian Brethren have long appreciated. It is, after all, the only service the Lord left us. It is manifestly the most important expression of Christian worship. And one of the interesting features of modern worship is the way in which so many of the newly rediscovered gifts of the Spirit are most naturally displayed at the communion. In denominations ranging from the Roman Catholic to the Pentecostal the eucharist has become the focus for singing in tongues, prophecies and healings. It is hardly surprising that the early Christians continued in the breaking of bread'. It was one of the great ways of being knit together into one body in Christ and nourished for the battle of Christian living in a pagan society. It still is. I find our own congregation, whose background is predominantly Protestant and evangelical, love the communion more than any other service. They would not willingly go back to the days when it was tucked away at 8.00 a.m. or after one of the other services as a pious postscript. These days it is held at one of the main services. When the church is very full we pass the loaf and the cup along the rows, thus enhancing the sense of unity. At other times we have an opportunity for those who so desire to come for counsel or the laying-on of hands when receiving communion. And generally there is quiet singing of modern songs of worship. There is also a growth of house communions in the area fellowship groups. These always seem to be the most meaningful and profitable of the group meetings. The apostolic emphasis on the eucharist is, then, not something I have always obeyed. But I do now, and I hope to go on discovering further depths in this most wonderful sacrament of our redemption which is both the means of grace and the hope of glory.

Chapter 5

Their motives and methods

This book arose from my being invited to give the Denman Lectures for the United Methodist Church in Miami in January 1978. I was fascinated to hear a bit about this remarkable man, Harry Denman. He was a layman, who remained unmarried all his days for Christ's sake. He was a man who used to possess only one suit and pair of shoes until he wore them out and replaced them. He was a man with no settled income and was liable to donate to anyone in need such money as might be given to him. He was supported by the gifts of God's people. He held meetings, but rarely advertised them. His speciality was personal evangelism. If invited to speak at a meeting he was apt to say to the person who met him at the railway station, 'Right, whom shall we go and visit first'? He would wander along the sea front to find lonely people to talk to. In his life he led many thousands of people to Jesus Christ. Why did he bother? Because he was a man of the same spirit as the early Christians. He was consumed with the same passion to spread the gospel.

That gospel so gripped Barnabas, a conservative, ecclesiastical landowner, that he sold his farm, gave up his money to the cause, and burnt himself out in the service of his Master: his speciality was rejoicing at other people's success and encouraging everybody in his path, including impossible characters like Saul of Tarsus.

That gospel so gripped Philip, a Greek-speaking (and probably Greek-living) businessman from Caesarea that he first turned into a church administrator and then discovered he had a gift for evangelism: his speciality was always to reach out to people beyond the pale, like Samaritans (whom nobody else would go near) and Ethiopian eunuchs. He also kept open house, and it must have been quite a place. It contained four daughters, all of whom had the gift of prophecy. Their fame reached far into the second century!

That gospel so gripped Peter that his mercurial character was changed into rocklike dedication. He found his prejudices of a lifetime melting away as he shared the good news of a Saviour with a type he had always been brought up to despise, the Gentile Cornelius. In so doing he broke all the laws of his church, and had no regrets. His speciality seems to have been widespread and assiduous travel for his Lord. You might find him in Jerusalem, Antioch, the fringes of Russia, or Rome.

That gospel so gripped Saul of Tarsus that he gave up his security, his intellectual arrogance (though not his intellectual competence), his status, his prospects, his finances—in order to be a lifelong evangelist, missionary, apologist, strategist and martyr for the Jesus he had once so vehemently repudiated.

That gospel so gripped unknown laymen that they went on a long safari from Jerusalem in order to chat informally to all they met about Jesus. Almost by mistake they founded the church which became the springboard for world evangelization, in Antioch on the Orontes, capital of Syria.

Why did they all bother?

Motives in evangelism

There need to be powerful motives if we are to pluck up courage to start this daunting task, where embarrassment has to be overcome, openings made and time sacrificed. There need to be powerful motives if we are not to give up in discouragement when we see little if any fruit from our efforts. As a matter of fact there are powerful motives, and the early Christians knew them and were moved by them. Here they are.

110

They bothered because of God's love

God so loved the world that he gave his only Son. He had only one Son, and that Son was a missionary. What is more, God's own love became implanted in the hearts of believers (Rom. 5:5) and so, not surprisingly, they began to share the heavenly Father's attitude to the lost.

They bothered because of Christ's command

In Matthew 28:18–20 we see the farewell words of Jesus to his disciples. He assures them that he has all power in heaven and earth. He promises that he will be with them until the end of the age. And then he gives them his parting instructions. They are to go into all the world and make disciples. They could claim his promises of power and presence only if they were obedient to that last command. We treat the last wishes of those we love very seriously. So did the early Christians: and this was Christ's last behest. Perhaps that is why they gave themselves so unremittingly to evangelism.

They bothered because of the Holy Spirit's thrust

The Spirit was given not to make us comfortable but to make us missionaries. The disciples were vaguely wondering when the end of the world would be, and Jesus told them that this was not their business. They were to await the coming of the Spirit who would empower them to move outwards in ever-widening ripples from Jerusalem to Judea, Samaria, and the uttermost parts of the earth (Acts 1:8). It was inconceivable to the early Christians that anyone could receive God's Holy Spirit without thereby being fired and equipped to speak for the Lord whenever opportunity knocked.

Do you notice that those first three motives for evangelism are all rooted in the nature of Almighty God? They supply a trinitarian basis for evangelism. We are called to share the good news, because God is like that. Evangelism is the outworking through Christians of the love of God the Son. It is the implementing by Christians of the thrust of God the Holy Spirit.

111

That is why they bothered. Because of the God who had disclosed himself to them. Isn't that enough? Well, it is not enough for most of us most of the time. We sit there and say 'Fine'—and pass the buck to somebody else. So the New Testament gives us other reasons why they bothered.

They bothered because of their responsibility

2 Corinthians 5:20 speaks of the Christian as Christ's ambassador who beseeches people on behalf of Christ to get reconciled with God. An ambassador represents his country in a foreign land, and is responsible for passing on his country's policies. If his life is unworthy people will not want to enquire about his country. If he keeps silent, they will not hear. He has a considerable responsibility as an ambassador. That responsibility is ours. We are Christ's embassy in a foreign and sometimes hostile land. He relies on us. As Paul reflects on it, he sees that God has taken us into partnership. 'We are labourers together with God' (1 Cor. 3:9). What if we fail? We are debtors, says the apostle Paul, both to the Greek and to the Jew (Rom. 1:14). What if we do not discharge our obligation? The answer is given in an apocryphal tale about what happened when Jesus returned to heaven after the ascension. He was greeted by the angelic host, and Gabriel asked him what plans he had made for continuing his work on earth. He replied, 'I have left behind eleven men, and have entrusted the task to them.' 'But what if they fail?' asked Gabriel. Jesus replied, 'If they fail—I have no other plan.'

They bothered because of their great privilege

What an amazing thing it is that God should make his appeal through us. What an astounding thing that he should entrust his precious jewel to our earthly vessels. But he does. Paul mulls it over in 2 Corinthians 4:1. There was every reason why he should lose heart, and play the coward in the light of all the pressures from within and opposition from without that came his way when he proclaimed the good news. Didn't the man ever take a rest? Didn't he ever lose heart?

Two things kept him from it, he tells us. For one thing he

recalled how he had received mercy. Blasphemer, persecutor that he was, he had been forgiven, accepted by the Lord, justified. And he never forgot it. When his heart grew cold, he would look back to the cross and see how costly his rescue had proved to his Lord. And that thought would nerve his sinews and restore his sagging zeal. It is very difficult to look at the crucified Saviour and say, 'So what? I don't care enough to tell others of what you have done.' The other thought that moved him was this: he had received 'this ministry'. He, Saul. It never ceased to amaze him that the privilege of representing the Lord should have been entrusted not to angels, not to kings and high politicians, but to forgiven sinners. The heavenly Father takes us into his family and gives us a share in the family business. It is a work from which we shall never be sacked and never need to retire. God has determined that he will only speak through the voice of reconciled sinners in reaching unreconciled sinners. What a privilege that is for us. I think the immensity of it struck Paul more and more as he got older. It brought him lower and lower in humility before his Saviour and Lord. In 1 Corinthians 15:9 he reckons that he is not worthy to be called an apostle because he had persecuted the church. But he has a lower estimate of himself by the time he writes Ephesians 3:7–9, where he is talking of the amazing privilege of telling Gentiles so that they can become fellow-heirs. He says 'to me who am *less than the least* of all Christians is this privilege given' (coining a word in his enthusiasm!). Lower still he goes as he reflects on this privilege, and by the time he discusses it in 1 Timothy 1:15 he sees himself as 'the chief of sinners'. But to the chief of sinners is given the privilege of telling other sinners about the Saviour. Throughout his life he gains a growing sense of the privilege of serving the Lord in evangelism; and with it goes a growing sense of his unworthiness.

They bothered because of other people's need

According to Ephesians 2:1 men and women without Christ are dead—their sin has cut them off from the life of God as effectively as death cuts man off from the life of his friends.

Though mentally, physically and emotionally alive, people are spiritually dead. There has been a great sense of this deadness, this absence of purpose and meaning, in recent years, as modern films, songs and plays have made so plain. Repeatedly we have been told that love is dead, fashion is dead, sex is dead, God is dead. That is where so many people around us are at, whereas we have found in Christ the elixir of life! What a responsibility rests upon us to share it. According to Jesus' own words and people's own assessment, society has lost its way, and man has an identity crisis. He does not know who he is, where he is going, or what there is to live for.

Now Jesus came to seek and to save the lost (Lk. 19:10). But people do not realize this. They think Christianity is about rules and churchgoing and obligations, and have no idea that Jesus can meet their deepest needs and aspirations. 'If our gospel is veiled, it is veiled to those who are lost' (2 Cor. 4:3). That is the realistic assessment of the situation. But why do they not see their predicament and turn to the only one who can get them out of it? Because 'the god of this world has blinded the minds of unbelievers, to prevent the light of the gospel of the glory of Christ from shining through to them.' Paul believed there was a great 'outside hindrance' to evangelism. The Enemy excels in propaganda, and blinds people's minds both to their need and to what Christ can do. Satan does not mind how nice they are, how good, how sincere or how religious, so long as he can prevent the truth of Jesus shining through to their minds and leading them to change sides. Such is the New Testament's understanding of the need of those without Christ. They saw evangelism as enabling people to 'escape from the snare of the devil, after being captured by him to do his will' (2 Tim. 2:26). We are not going to be much use in evangelism unless we are prepared to reckon with this satanic opposition. Like Jesus before them, they saw Satan as the usurper prince of this world, taking the place God should have in people's esteem. To be sure, they knew that their Lord was mightier; 'The God who said, "Let light shine out of darkness," has shone in our hearts to give the light of the knowledge of the glory of God in the face of Jesus Christ' (2

Cor. 4:6)—and if he has done it for us he can do it for others through us. But not if we fail to engage in the intense spiritual battle by giving ourselves to prayer. For people are, as Paul put it 'without hope and without God in the world' (Eph. 2:12). Now it is very hard to believe this, especially of charming people and our own personal friends. But I am sure that once it dawned on me that such people around me were lost, were basically under the control of the Enemy who was determined to keep them from Christ—then it was that the passion for evangelism was kindled in my heart. That was over twenty years ago, and it is still one of the most powerful levers on my apathetic will to drive me out in loving service.

This is, of course, a most unfashionable doctrine, but it is unquestionably the teaching of the New Testament. It talks of two realms: darkness and light. It talks of two powers: the power of Satan and of God. It talks of two rulers: the God of this world and Almighty God. It talks about two ways: the broad way which leads to destruction or the narrow way which leads to life. It talks about two choices: for Christ or against him. It talks about two groupings: wheat and tares, wise and foolish, in or out of the great supper, with Christ or without Christ. *There is no middle ground.* Now it was that which drove Paul and the other early missionaries into such unremitting service. They had a clear, unromantic recognition of the appalling need of those who were out of touch with God. General Booth, founder of the Salvation Army, was stung into the same recognition by an atheist who said, 'If I believed what you Christians believe I would crawl across England on my hands and knees, if need be, to tell men about it.' Once you have been gripped by the need of those who do not know your Lord Jesus Christ, you will need no other motivation to spread the good news with every power at your disposal.

They bothered because it brought joy

Those early Christians found that there was no joy like it. Listen to 1 Thessalonians 1:5–6. 'Our gospel came to you not only in word, but also in power and in the Holy Spirit and with full conviction ... You received the word in much affliction,

115

with joy inspired by the Holy Spirit.' The joy in the hearts of the converts was there in the missionaries too. 'For what is our joy? Is it not you'? (2:19). Or listen to the enthusiastic opening of 1 John 1—John's passionate personal testimony to the Word made flesh ('which he have seen with our eyes . . . and handled with our hands').Why did he proclaim it? 'So that you may have fellowship with us and with Jesus, that our joy may be full.' Or again, as 3 John 4 so simply puts it, 'I have no greater joy than to know that my children walk in the truth.' He is quite right. There is no joy like it. Last week I was given a surprise. I was met off the aeroplane in Toronto by a Ghanaian girl whom I led to Christ seven years ago in Ghana. It was a tremendous joy for both of us. Last night I was at a meeting when a Chinaman came to see me. I had had the joy of introducing him to the Lord five years ago. It was a wonderful surprise, for this was Vancouver and I had last seen him in Derby! But the joy was pure and deep. I believe it is the greatest joy in the world. And quite honestly, that is one of the reasons why I engage in evangelism. The early Christians seem to have done it for this reason, too. There is no joy like it.

Those are seven of the motives which burnt themselves into the minds and consciences of the early disciples. They are worth pondering. If they catch light in us, we will be at this business of sharing the good news until our death bed. If not, no consideration of methods (to which we shall now turn) will do any good. The biggest problem in evangelism is not to find methods (where there is a will there is always a way) but to motivate. And if the example of the holy Trinity, the privilege and responsibility laid upon us, the need of those without Christ and the sheer joy of serving him in this way do not move us, I do not know what will.

Methods in evangelism

I am not sure that it is very important to talk about methods. For one thing the early Christians did not come up with anything extraordinary in this area. For another it would be futile to suppose that Christians do not evangelize because they do not know what to do. It is not ignorance but motivation which is the trouble. Today's church is full of methods of evangelism (together with training courses and congresses) but not a great deal gets done. There is not enough fire in the belly. Once the fire is there, people discover methods. I find that in our congregation the best evangelists are the folk who have been Christians the shortest time—and have not yet been spoiled by going to courses on evangelism or reading the appropriate manuals of instruction! I remember vividly a Texan describing the way he drove through a dust storm. He shut the windows, blocked every crevice that he knew of in the car, and kept driving, driving, driving. But it made no difference. The dust and sand, driven by the wind, kept getting through. It is like that with Christians. If the wind of the Spirit is driving them, they will get through however few methods they know or however seemingly impenetrable the opposition. However, the approaches the early Christians adopted are significant and stimulating. Here, as a sample, are eight which most local churches could take up, if they had the mind, even though their resources were very slight.

They went for every-member witness

That is the biggest difference between the New Testament church and our own. Their responsibility of bearing witness to Jesus rested fairly and squarely upon every single member. You find it in the odd byways of the New Testament: Jude urges his readers in graphic terms to 'save some, by snatching them out of the fire' (verse 23). Timothy, though naturally timid and not an evangelist, is nevertheless bidden to 'do the work of an evangelist' and 'be urgent in season and out of season' (2 Tim. 4:5, 2). But you find it everywhere. In 1 Thessalonians 1:8 Paul rejoices that the word of God has sounded forth from those newly fledged Thessalonian Christians, and their faith in God has spread like wildfire. And in Acts 8:1, 4 we find the Jerusalem leaders shut up in fear in an upper room while the common believers were scattered by a persecution springing from the death of Stephen. What did they do? They went everywhere

117

spreading the good news. It was every-member ministry in those days. Evangelism was the spontaneous chattering of good news. It was engaged in naturally, continuously, easily and joyfully by Christians wherever they went. Harnack justly remarks that the mission of the early church was in fact accomplished to a very large extent by informal missionaries. Christians would wander from hamlet to hamlet, village to village, in order to win fresh converts to their Lord.

Is that not staggeringly different from our own day? These days evangelism is spasmodic (if it happens at all), expensive, minister-dominated, and is dependent upon the skills of the resident evangelist or visiting specialist. That is exceedingly foolish. I remember going to Manchester and preaching in a remarkable church that was full to overflowing. Many people responded to the challenge of the gospel, and stayed behind afterwards to express in tangible form their commitment to Christ. I had rarely seen such a response, and I wanted to know what lay behind it. But as I talked to the new believers I soon found out. When asked if they had anybody they thought could help them in the early days of their discipleship, without exception they pointed to some self-effacing companion who was a few yards away. 'Yes, there is Bill. He invited me along. In fact he has been talking to me for some time about becoming a Christian. He will be able to help me out.' That was the sort of response. And it pointed to the secret of that church's dynamism: they did not rely on the skills of their able minister, but they each recognised their responsibility to live and work and speak for Jesus. That is how the gospel spreads. If you want evangelism in your church, do not hire a famous preacher. Build up the congregation for informal witness. And the church will grow.

They worked outwards from the centre

Had not Jesus stressed that they were to set out on their task 'beginning from Jerusalem', just where they were? Had he not concentrated in his own work on twelve men? From those twelve we find 120 in the days before Pentecost, then 3,000 on the day itself, and from then on the faith spread in ever-
118

widening ripples from Jerusalem towards Rome. Surely there is a message here for the activity-prone modern church. We do not get from the early church the idea of visiting all round the suburbs in the hope that something will happen with someone. That has its place, of course, but it is far less important and effective than working to get the centre of the church really hot. It is not difficult to discern from the conclusion of Acts 2 and 4 that this was a priority to the early Christians. Their fellowship was vibrant; we find them sharing homes, praising God, praying till the place shook, engaging in street evangelism, loving and caring for one another, learning from one another. They were so warm with the Holy Spirit's fire that people were sucked in as by a vortex. God added daily to the church those whom he was saving. In the three years I have been in Oxford I have known two periods where God added daily to the church. People would just come and knock on the door and ask how to become Christians. Some of them one had never set eyes on before. I do not know why it does not happen more often. But I do know it can happen. And I think it does so when there is warmth, love, vitality and expectancy at the centre of church life. If we really want to reach out with the gospel, we must attend to life at the centre. If that is not open to the Spirit of God, if it is not warm and caring, then you are wasting your time going round the highways and hedges.

They concentrated on the 'godfearing fringe'

There was a very large fringe on the edge of most synagogues in the first century. Many people drew the line at being circumcised and joining the Jewish people, but all the same enjoyed their worship, admired their monotheism and were struck by their Scriptures. The record of the Acts shows that it was in this fringe that the Christian evangelists were conspicuously successful. Time and again we find them preaching evangelistically in just this type of situation.

Acts 13 is a model for preaching in church where a large number of those present are occasional fringe members (of the Christmas, Easter and Harvest variety). Paul began precisely where people were (verse 16). He showed how relevant Scripture was, and that it had come true (17f.). He told them of God at work in the contemporary situation (23), and this always attracts interest. He preached Jesus, not a doctrine (38f.), and showed how Jesus could meet their deepest needs that could not be dealt with in any other way (39). There was a touch of personal testimony, but not enough to be sickly (31). He also struck the note of appeal to his listeners (26) and a warning about the seriousness of the issues involved (41). As they went out, we read, the people begged that these things might be told them the next sabbath. Hardly surprising. It took them by storm, and sensing the reality, they wanted to know more.

Opportunities abound among our fringe, if only we will take them. Christian Business Men's Lunches (where a business man speaks of what Jesus Christ can mean in business and of what Christ has done for him personally) can have an enormous impact. Weekends away camping. Wine and cheese parties. I have known sessions in public houses to be extremely productive and even to have led to conversions on the spot. Meetings for sportsmen with a Christian sportsman speaking —or for politicians, or any other obvious grouping. Work on the fringe is profitable. Especially strive and pray for the conversion of those whose spouses are committed Christians. God will already be at work in such families, challenging, pleading. Capitalize on it. It is particularly important to find an approach that appeals to the men. Even in this women's-lib. age it is normally the man in the family who makes the running. Win him and there is a good chance that you will win the family. Concentrate on the women and children and he will be confirmed in his prejudice that religion is for the wife and kids and nothing to do with a tough man like him! Go for the man. A church needs to be very sure what it is doing before it lays on lots of sectional meetings for women and a Sunday School for the children where no attempt is made to involve the dads. It is laying up trouble for the future, because as soon as he is or feels himself to be 'grown up' the son will disappear from the scene, sure that like Dad he has outgrown such boring stuff. For ever afterwards he will be sufficiently innoculated with a little watered-down religion to immunize him effectively against the real thing.

And just one more point while in this area of working among the fringe. You get a lot further by outreach than you do by indrag. In most churches what we call outreach is nothing of the sort: it is a blatant attempt to get the fringer on to your ground. It is indrag. But is that wise? Is he not going to feel a lot more at home on neutral ground, or, better still, on his own ground? You are likely to put him much more at ease by speaking at a home meeting in his house than by dragging him off to some evangelistic service where he feels he is a sitting duck being shot at by the preacher. Outreach as opposed to indrag. It is worth pondering.

They ran a lot of home meetings

It went on in Jason's house (Acts 17:5) in Justus's house (18:7), Philip's house (21:8) and so on. Sometimes it was a meeting for prayer (12:12), sometimes a fellowship meeting (20:7). Sometimes it was a Holy Communion (2:46), sometimes a follow-up meeting (5:42), sometimes an evangelistic day study conference (28:17ff.), sometimes an impromptu gathering (16:32) and occasionally they found a house full of seekers, just waiting to hear the good news (10:22).

The home is a priceless asset. It is informal and relaxed. It makes participation easy. The leader is not six feet above contradiction and there is no temptation to put on a performance. So use the homes of the people in the congregation. Use them for home Bible studies, for training groups, for a basis for street evangelism, for baptism preparation classes (with lay members of the congregation doing the preparation). Put on evangelistic supper and coffee parties; use slides or filmstrips as a change. A group of people I have just been with have found evangelistic Bible studies exceedingly fruitful: they merely asked their friends to come and read Mark's Gospel through with them in a six-week session. They did not have to come to church. They did not commit themselves to doing anything subsequently. They did

121

not have to *believe* Mark, only to come with an open mind to read and discuss. I met some of the converts won through that approach. It works: because the Word of God is alive and powerful, and if we can expose people to its radiation things are inclined to happen to them. Stupidly we have the idea that nobody will want to read it and are almost ashamed to commend the Scriptures to people! Yes, the home meeting is invaluable. Paul recalled how he supplemented his public teaching with house-to-house work (Acts 20:20), and Richard Baxter's effectiveness only really began when he paid attention to home meetings. He confessed, 'I find more signs of success in this work than in all my public preaching.'

The church in the first century grew rapidly and effectively without the aid of two of our most prized evangelistic assets, mass evangelism and evangelism in the church building. They used the home. Why don't we learn from them?

They loved to discuss on neutral ground

It might be with Jews in a hired house in Rome (Acts 28: 17ff.). It might be when on trial in court (Acts 22 and 2 Tim. 4:16–17) just as the Russian Christian Georgi Vins has done in our own day. It might be occasioned by meeting a beggar in the street (Acts 3) or deliberately setting up a situation for dialogue and proclamation such as Paul did when he took over the school of Tyrannus in the hours when that gentleman did not require it because, so one ancient manuscript tells us, it was siesta time in the middle of the day (Acts 19:9).

I doubt if we use this method today with anything like the vigour and enthusiasm that we should. I discovered it by accident, when preaching in Cambridge at the Senate House on 'Jesus the Radical', and comparing and contrasting his radicalism with that of Chairman Mao. After the main address we had three quarters of an hour of dialogue before a final five minutes of challenge to radical discipleship. By instinct and precedent I would not have had this dialogue time in an overtly evangelistic situation: would it not destroy the atmosphere? Far from it, I discovered. The response to Christ at that meeting was enormous. All the literature on beginning life

122

with Christ disappeared in a flash, and people were entrusting their lives to our Lord as a result for some weeks to come. It taught me an important lesson. Since then I have done a lot of dialogue presentation in missions, in open air situations and in public lectures. It is always profitable. I think of a crowded debate in one British university when some of us opposed the motion that 'This House believes that Christianity is founded on a lie'. The testimony from the floor of the debate was so powerful, the difference in the lives of those who spoke so marked, that the outcome was a foregone conclusion and the anti-Christian lobby on that occasion gained a mere handful of votes. But the significant thing was the amount of discussion about Christ that went on throughout that night as a result of the debate. The atheistic secretary of the Debating Union sat up all night studying the resurrection of Jesus. Nowadays in our own church we do this sort of thing. I have recently debated the reality of Christ's incarnation with one of the authors of *The Myth of God Incarnate*, and the utopian dream with Tony Benn, the British Minister of Energy. Why do we fear such occasions? Do we really believe that in Jesus Christ we have the final truth about God and man? If so, why should we not fearlessly discuss it and debate it with those who think it is erroneous? The early Christians did. Philosophers like Justin continued the open-air tradition of the earliest disciples. It still remains a viable mode of evangelism today. It is not everybody's gift, but it has its own charm and forthrightness, particularly if done sensitively, with humour, and if possible illuminated by a visual aid. Recently we have used a group who have been developing dance as a mode of worship, and with them a singing group. This is particularly effective in a festive situation, such as the boat races at Oxford when everyone is happy and relaxed down by the river and something too 'heavy' would be inappropriate. Another dialogue situation which is proving itself these days is the gathering of a few friends into a room to discuss some important issues of human life and destiny. One person starts off with a few minutes of Christian conviction on the subject. The discussion is then taken up by others, and the fifty-fifty mixture of Christians and non-

123

Christians will ensure not only that there is adequate input from the Christian perspective but also that when people want to break up and take the matter further in private it is natural to move off in pairs, Christian and non-Christian together.

There are many other ways of holding dialogue. Some churches hire the town hall and put on debates on controversial issues between a known Christian and a known humanist or communist. Our own church runs groups called Agnostics Anonymous where those who are emphatically not Christians can come and discuss the faith with Christian believers and see where the argument leads. Recently I was in a remarkable house, bought and equipped by a Christian church, where people off the street are in a habit of dropping in for food, company and someone to talk to. A team of fifteen from the church man it on each occasion, and the atmosphere is warm, bathed in prayer, and natural. Glancing round the room, full as it was of a very mixed bag, including a couple of prostitutes, several convicts, boys from a detention centre, middle-class people, and those whose minds had been blown by heroin, one saw friendly and animated conversation going on all over the place. They were not just talking about the weather—nor were they thrusting their views down the throats of those who did not want to know. But the mere existence of this loving, well-appointed Christian restaurant, so different from anything anybody present had ever seen, made questions about what lay behind it inevitable. Thus it was only too easy for a group of devoted and delightful Christians on the team to chat informally and naturally about their Lord. I met two people who had that week found Christ in such a context. It is a costly project to mount in terms of manpower, organization and time: over 120 people in that particular church are involved. But should we not be putting ourselves out in the cause of the gospel, cost what it may?

They wrote and used literature

I think we may safely infer this from two factors. First, they made extensive use of the Greek translation of the Old Testament Scriptures in commending the Lord Jesus. We find it in the sermons recorded in Acts—a constant frame of reference to the Old Testament. We find it in the assumptions made by the writers of the New Testament Letters that their readers know the Old Testament with some sureness of touch. The other factor which makes it certain Christians used and disseminated literature is the existence of Gospels and Letters. Mark started a completely new literary genre under the spell of Jesus. It was a brilliant idea, to gather together various elements of oral tradition and perhaps some rudimentary written sources and weave them together into a continuous narrative, whose aim would not be biographic but evangelistic. He tells us nothing about the personal characteristics of Jesus, nothing about thirty years of his life. And he is highly selective about using material from his ministry. But he wanted to show who Jesus was (almost every short paragraph in his Gospel is about the person of Jesus), and how he could transform the lives of those with whom he came in contact. Actually, Mark may not only have invented the Gospel form with its strong if implicit challenge to discipleship, but also the papyrus codex as well. The Jews used long scrolls for their holy books; but these were cumbersome to use. The Greeks used our book form, the codex, for their literary works; but generally made use of treated skins, such as vellum, and this was expensive. The early Christians seem to have been among the first, if not the very first, to have used a codex made of papyrus for their publications. The advantages are obvious. It was easy to read, easy to find a place in, easy to hide—and wonderfully cheap to produce. The greater proportion of papyrus codices know to us from the second and third centuries are Christian. It is probably a Christian invention, and may well have gone back to Mark.

However that may be, it is clear that the early disciples of Jesus made use of literature. This included the dissemination of the Old Testament Scriptures, Gospels (produced by amateur scribes on commonplace materials at a cheap price) and, of course, the valuable tool of letter-writing to individuals and churches of which there is such striking evidence in the New Testament. If we look beneath the surface in our New

Testaments it is possible to discern, with varying degrees of certainty, other written material of which they made use. 'Q' is the symbol New Testament scholars use to denote the sayings of Jesus common to Matthew and Luke but absent from Mark. It is almost universally agreed that this was a written source, in Greek or Aramaic, for early preachers to have and carry round in their missions. They would refer to it when an audience asked them what sort of things this Jesus of theirs taught. There also seem to be fragments of early creeds and hymns embodied here and there within the Letters, and perhaps the outlines of a common approach to the problems of building up new converts, guarding against false teaching, and instilling an ethic based on love. In the second century, also, you got 'apologies' being written, primarily to defend Christianity against the charges brought against it, and also to win people to the faith. Perhaps the two-volume Luke-Acts is the prototype of all such apologies: its emphasis on the sinlessness of Jesus, the innocence of Christians (confirmed in trial after trial in Acts) and the importance of responding to the good news (hence the many evangelistic sermons recorded in Acts) would all fit such a possibility.

This variety of literature has an important message for us in these days when the media are so much more widespread and powerful. In America there is a most impressive and popular coast-to-coast television network run by Christians and bringing a clear Christian message. But in Britain there is nothing of the sort. You cannot 'buy time', and the majority of television programmes concerned with Christianity are feeble and inconclusive discussions. There is almost no straight proclamation of the good news by those who believe it passionately. As a result, the Briton who regarded religious instruction in school as an occasional joke is confirmed in the belief that God can safely be ignored and probably does not even exist.

It is much the same on the literature front. An enormous amount of literature is produced by Christians for Christians, but attempts to put the message in terms of the man in the street are remarkably few. We have little if any good Christian literature for the worker who looks at his daily paper rather than reads it. We have few if any successful Christian films. We have made little if any impact on the chain stores in matching porn with Christian material—at least in Britain, though in North America they have been much more successful. Christian material is not normally to be found in the general bookshops: it hives away in the local Christian bookshop—if there is one. How can we really believe that we are the salt of the earth if the salt is kept so firmly in the salt cellar?

I believe that in the media we have an incalculable instrument for the presentation of the Christian faith. Certain publishers, certain television and radio stations, certain churches have become aware of its potential and are doing something about it. How are we doing, personally? Can you write in a gripping way? Then why not bend your skill to communicating the most profound truths in the most simple terms that can reach the man in the street? I assure you there will be a publisher! Have you a small library of Christian books? If not, why not? If so, do you lend them to your non-Christian friends? Lending is better than giving, on the whole: it provides an opportunity for you to discuss the content of the book after he has read it. Could you run a weekly or monthly column in the local newspaper? There is no harm in trying the editor; he can only refuse—or say 'Yes'. Could you run a coffee morning in your house at which you invite the manager of the church bookstall to run a display? Could you run a bookstall yourself at the next fair in town, or at the weekly market? The opportunities are limitless. And people are often more spiritually hungry than we think. Use the written word: it reaches more people and lasts longer than the spoken word does. We are fools to neglect it.

They engaged in 'missionary journeys'

If we are to judge by the Acts, it was not uncommon for churches to encourage small groups of three or four to go out on a short or more extended missionary journey. We know from the church historian Eusebius that this sort of thing continued for the next hundred years and more, as believers

127

went from town to town and village to village charged with the news of their Lord's love. The Acts bears profuse testimony to this method of advance, and so does one of the earliest sub-apostolic writings, the *Didache*, which has a good deal to say about wandering teachers and delegates from other churches. It provides some amusing tests of genuineness for these wandering teachers. If a man orders a meal while under the inspiration of God's Spirit, he must not eat of it himself! If a wandering teacher stays too long he is to be sent away: he is abusing the hospitality! Clearly, these 'missionary journeys' were one of the main ways in which the faith was spread.

I think we have a good deal to learn in this respect. There is a great value in teams of witness going out from one church to another, or to an 'open' situation which may not be organized by a church at all. The 'mission' to a parish or university has long been traditional, but often this has been a one-man-band, as people are dragged off by their friends to 'hear the preacher'. I have now set my face firmly against this sort of evangelism. I believe in the concept of the team. Nearly always a personal invitation to me gets turned into one for a team from our church, and many good things emerge from it. One is the unity and partnership which develops among the team. One is the mutual learning as we plan our respective parts in the project. One is the unanimity with which different members of the team bear their respective witness to Jesus. One is the good which team members do in the homes where they stay, if the visit is for a night or longer. Another is the unspoken visual emphasis given to the fact that we cannot live the Christian life in isolation but are part of a family, a body. Another benefit is the way in which the less experienced members of the team learn from the more experienced. After all, our most effective learning is not normally gained from books or lectures but from partnership, in action, with more experienced people. We learn, in fact, by doing. This is how Paul trained a Timothy, a Titus, a Luke. This is one of the great ways of training fellow workers. It could be widely used in the churches and the para-church organizations.

We in Oxford use it at three levels. Each year our church

128

mounts a large mission, with about eighty participants, in some church or churches in another part of the country. This is carefully prepared for at both ends. There is centralized preaching, masses of house meetings, sessions in pubs and factories and generally a lot of work among senior schoolchildren. Members of the team have a teaching and worship session each morning, and are all engaged on the job in the afternoon and evening. The sheer impact of this enthusiasm and dedication speaks volumes. The homes where team members stay are usually greatly blessed. A good many people come into a vital Christian experience, and the team is as encouraged as the local church. There is joy in heaven, we are told, when folk repent and find the Saviour: well, there is joy on earth as well.

In addition to this longer event (ten days or two weeks) we have found another type of team ministry in evangelism to be useful. We run a training course each year in various sides of basic Christian leadership. At the end of this course (which takes three months or so), we go on a mini-mission. We arrange with some local parish who would like to have us, and agree to go over on three successive Wednesdays to lead (or join with their local leaders in leading) a number of house meetings. These meetings are attended by the same two or three folk from our church on each of the three evenings, and the subject considered is some very central one: 'What is a Christian?' was the most recent. In this way some headway is made on Wednesday evenings, and it is complemented by the Sunday worship, which is largely led by members of our team for those three Sundays. The singing group and maybe dance group take part; drama may be used; testimony and interview are almost sure to figure in the services, and on the last of the three Sundays there is a definite challenge to commitment. When people respond, they are counselled by members of the team. It may then be that the local minister asks one or two of our team to come back for a few weeks to run a follow-up course for those who have found Christ during the past three weeks. Or it may be that some young people have been converted, and they need help in running a group to contain them in the early days, while other local leaders are being

129

prepared for the task. This sort of 'missionary journey' is eminently practical: no accommodation is needed. It has a limited duration. It involves only three Sundays and three weeknights. It is flexible and easy to adapt. It can be done evangelistically or to teach stewardship or some other chosen subject, or in the interests of spiritual renewal in the parish.

A third way in which we find it helpful for members of the congregation to both be encouraged and bring encouragement to others is the one-night stand. A team prepares a combined evening and goes out in response to an invitation. Each one speaks for Christ. The impact is far more total (if less polished) than if it had been brought by one member only. The members of the team unconsciously bear witness to the uniting effect of Christ by the way they relate together, and that is noticed. They are also available to talk with people afterwards, so far more ground is covered than in the case of a one-man speaker.

Here are just three of many ways in which this team principle can be used in evangelism. Blessing and growth emerge at both ends: in fact, it is hard to speak of 'ends', for the receiving and giving is mutual. There is an enrichment all round, just such as Paul knew his visit to Rome would produce—'mutually encouraged by each other's faith, both yours and mine' (Rom. 1:12). As with the early Christians, we should make use of teams; we should stay a short time only in a place; and we should be backed and supported in prayer—and transport—by our own home church, to whom we should bring back news of encouragements and items for prayer. This is how Paul and Barnabas returned to their sending church, Antioch, and 'gathered the church together and declared all that God had done with them, and how he had opened a door of faith' to unbelievers (Acts 14:27).

They relied on personal talks

The last method I propose to mention brings us back to the main thrust of chapter 3. Personal conversation was the main method by which the gospel spread in the earliest days. Little groups would discuss it in the streets; women would chatter about it at the public laundry. Folk would go and visit their friends (just as Ananias visited Paul and brought him such release) and thus the word spread and so did the number of those who through that message came to entrust their lives to Christ.

Philip is, I suppose, the classic example to us here. He does not seem to have been used to all this evangelism business: he was after all, appointed to look after the soup kitchens of the early church. But once he had found the joy of introducing others to Christ there was no stopping him. His approach to the Ethiopian eunuch is exemplary. First, he was absolutely right with God. The Spirit of the Lord had indicated that he should go apart into the desert, that he should approach this particular man, that he should in due course leave him—and he obeyed. He was so finely attuned to the Lord that he discerned—and followed—the direction in which he was being led (Acts 8:26, 29, 39). He was humble enough to leave a flourishing church situation in Samaria where he was the star figure and ask a man of a different colour, a different nationality and class, if he could be of any service to him. He had the enthusiasm to start a conversation in the heat of the day in the desert, and the sensitivity to approach the man in a way that evoked a warm and natural response (8:29ff.). He was tactful enough first to listen, then to discern the right approach in the circumstances, and only then to offer his services. No wonder he was asked to sit alongside the Ethiopian in his chariot. No wonder that before long, by using those scriptures that the man happened to be studying, he was able to lead the man to Christ and to baptism.

Most of us find opening conversations about Christian things the most difficult part of all. How on earth is one to get started in a natural sort of way? I believe this incident has several indicators for us. We, like Philip, must be in vital touch with the Lord. Otherwise, we will not sense his leading towards the individual he wants us to help, nor how to approach him if we do stumble across him. I am certain I miss many opportunities through being too distracted, too busy, too loosely attached to my Lord, to hear what he is trying to say to me. I know, too, that like Philip I have to be obedient. If I am

131

saying 'No' to God over anything in my life at the moment, he will not and cannot use me. Disobedience often makes me miss opportunities. So does pride. I rush foolishly into a conversation without waiting to listen and assess as Philip did. Humility is not only very attractive (who of us actually likes the brash salesman—which is what evangelistically minded Christians often appear to be?), but it is essential if we are to help the other person at that point where he will welcome help. Philip shows us how to take the natural opening. The man was sitting reading aloud from Isaiah 53. Well, our contacts will not always be as obliging as that. But it does stress the lesson that we must begin at the point of felt need. Is not that exactly how Jesus approached the palsied man (Mk. 2), or the blind man (Jn. 9), or the Samaritan woman (Jn. 4), or the woman taken in adultery (Jn. 8)? And one of the best ways of finding out where someone lives, spiritually speaking, is to ask him a question. Many Christians are finding that the use of a simple questionnaire is not only deemed acceptable by most people (if courteously approached); it also leads to most useful results. Questions such as, 'What do you understand by a Christian?' 'Do you think Jesus Christ can be encountered today?', 'Does faith in Christ spoil or enrich someone's enjoyment of life?', 'Why do you think that in an age of increasing education and affluence crime and dissatisfaction seem to be rising so fast?', can be calculated to open up profitable lines of conversation which can lead into a serious talk about Christ. One of the most effective evangelistic methods in America is based on the work of Dr Kennedy at Coral Ridge. His way is to ask one or two very simple but devastating questions such as, 'If you died tonight would you be confident of going to heaven?' followed up by, 'If you died tonight, why should God let you into his heaven?' If sensitively and flexibly used, the question method (and the joy of it is that you can devise your own, to suit your own personality) is one of the most natural ways of turning the conversation into profitable channels.

Another approach used in the New Testament a good deal is to point to some unusual mark of God's presence and use this as a way in for the gospel. This is how Peter and John in Acts 3 made capital of the healing of the man lame from birth. I met recently a woman healed from a terminal, and fully documented, brain tumour in answer to prayer some ten years ago. The healing plus her testimony to Jesus made a most powerful adjunct to lively and wholehearted worship by God's people and underlined the evangelistic preaching in a memorable way. The total impact of the evening led several people to entrust themselves to Jesus Christ.

Another approach used in New Testament times was to begin with an obvious need and work from there. I think of Paul making the impending shipwreck a chance to point to the overruling hand of God. I think of him dealing with the demon-possessed medium who followed him around at Philippi. Needs such as loneliness, the death of a loved one, deep disappointment, marriage, birth of a child are all occasions where signs of transcendence can so easily break in. At 5 o'clock the other morning I was awakened by a man who had broken into my room and was looking for something to steal. He did not need to be told be was guilty, but as we worked backwards from the situation to what prompted it, and began to unravel the sorrow and rejection which had characterized his life, he wanted to know if there was any hope for such as he. I tried to meet his need at two levels. The first was to see that he got food and shelter and a caring Christian community who could help him towards employment. The second was to get to the root of all the contradictions in his life, and come back as a prodigal to the Father's house from which he had run away. This made admirable sense to him. It was a very natural opening, even if at a somewhat early hour!

Sometimes a play on words gets a good conversation started. I have already mentioned the ambiguous word 'be saved' which the Philippian jailer used when his jail was tumbling down in ruins at the earthquake (Acts 16:30). Paul took that up and used the word in a much deeper sense: 'Believe in the Lord Jesus, and you will be saved.' If we listen sensitively to the cry of the heart which underlies so many comments made to us, we will be able to take those words, from time to time, and use them in a deeper sense—and so, perhaps, begin a conversation that has depth.

But the easiest way of all to start a conversation about Christ, arguably the most effective, is to be so full of the Lord that you can't help overflowing. Just as people in love can scarcely help themselves (it keeps bubbling out), so the first missionaries seemed to radiate joy. And people wanted to know why. At Thessalonica, for example, it was the mixture of joy and confidence that led to the spread of the message (1 Thes. 1:6). It was the joy of Jesus that led Paul and Silas to sing hymns at midnight in a filthy Philippian prison when their feet were fast in the stocks. This inevitably flowed over into telling about Jesus the moment opportunity offered. When people see that we have found treasure in Christ, and are not ashamed to talk about it, the questions come thick and fast and we are into conversations about the Lord before we know what is happening.

Personal conversation is the best way of evangelism. It is natural, it can be done anywhere, it can be done by anyone. It is a shared experience, when both learn and both teach. Unlike much preaching it hits the mark. Christ is the road that leads to God, and the early Christians were so keen proclaiming him and his resurrection that they could be misunderstood by the Athenians as preaching two new deities, Healer ('Jesus') and Resurrection ('Anastasis'). The very fact that they could so be misunderstood makes it very plain where their emphasis lay. Yes, the living Christ is the way to God, but there are many routes to Christ: as many as there are conversations and conversationalists. It was to this task of conversing naturally about Jesus that the early Christians addressed themselves, and in so doing have set us an example which we are curiously reluctant to follow.

GUIDES TO CONFERENCE CENTRES
TRACTS
TAPES
AUDIO-VISUAL AIDS
BIG MEETINGS GUIDES *
FILM PROJECTORS
EAFLETS
WITH CARE
LOUDSPEAKERS
WORLD EVANGELISM LTD
I'm sure I've forgotten Something...

Chapter 6

The architect of their success

We may make use of all the methods adopted by the early Christians: we may be fired by their motivation. But unless we have the power of the Holy Spirit we shall achieve nothing at all. The whole New Testament unites to tell us that evangelism is the work of the Spirit of God in and through us. God's Spirit is the prime agent of mission in God's people to God's world. All the early Christians were sure about that.

The agency of the Spirit in evangelism

There is a delightful passage in John 15:26 where Jesus says, in effect, 'I will send the Spirit, and he will bear witness to me.' I can just imagine the disciples thinking, 'That would be very nice!' Jesus' next words destroyed their illusion of an easy time: 'You also shall bear witness.' The Spirit and witness-bearing go together.

It is much the same story in Mark 13:10f. Before the end comes, the gospel must first be preached to the nations. And the disciples will be involved in this mission: it will not be easy. But the Holy Spirit will guide them what they should say when they are arraigned for their faith and called upon to bear witness. The Spirit and witness-bearing go together.

Luke records precisely the same emphasis. 'You shall receive power when the Holy Spirit comes upon you, and you shall be my witnesses . . .' (Acts 1:8).

We have already seen how Paul reminds the Thessalonians of the same thing. 'Our gospel came to you not only in word, but also in power and in the Holy Spirit and with full conviction.' The missionaries did the witnessing, but the Holy Spirit gave the power and produced the conviction in the hearers.

We shall not be surprised to see the same stress in 1 Peter 1:12, for the pattern is uniform in all the main strands of the New Testament teaching. He recalls his readers to those who preached the good news to them through the Holy Spirit sent from heaven. As always, the initiative and the power for mission come from the Lord who is Spirit.

And as the story of the earliest church unfolds in Acts, I see a very humbling thing. It is the Spirit of God who initiates evangelism, not the apostles. It is the Spirit who first nerves Peter to preach the good news in Jerusalem (chapter 2). It is the Spirit who leads Stephen to break out of the narrow confines of law-keeping and temple worship to reach the Hellenists (6:3, 5, 10; 7:55). It is the Spirit who brings those untouchables into the church, first the Samaritans, then the Ethiopian eunuch (chapter 8) then the Gentile godfearers like Cornelius (10:19, 44) and finally the complete pagans (14:46ff.). It is the Spirit who leads the Antioch church, while at worship, to send out Paul and Barnabas on that first missionary journey (13:2) from which they returned to report that the Lord 'opened the door of faith to the Gentiles' (14:27). Need I go on?

The bishops and ministers cannot provide power for evangelism. They need it as much as anyone else. The various boards for evangelism in the churches cannot provide that power, however good their organization and resource material. Only the Holy Spirit of God has the power to drive us out in loving self-sacrificial service. Only he can keep us humble and trustful and obedient. Only he can wing our words to help others into newness of life.

The role of the spirit in evangelizing

At every stage we are dependent on the Spirit in this work of passing on the good news. For not only does the Spirit thrust us out in evangelism and lead us in it to the place where he, like a good general, knows that we will be effective. The Spirit is also the prime mover in the hearts of those who hear: in five ways particularly.

It is the Spirit who shows someone his need of entering into God's family. 'When the Spirit comes, he will convict the world of sin' (John 16:8), and he does just that. You can speak as eloquently as the archangel Gabriel. You can preach with the power of John the Baptist. But unless the Holy Spirit convicts the hearer of his own need, that this message applies to him, nothing you say will have any effect. The whole mysterious area of conviction of sin lies in the supreme and unique control of the Holy Spirit.

Precisely the same is true when someone begins to fall under the 'spell of Jesus. It is the role of the Spirit to make Jesus attractive to people. 'He will bear witness to me ... he will glorify me ... he will take what is mine and declare it to you.' That was what Jesus promised (Jn. 15:26; 16:14f.). And the Spirit has been doing it ever since. There never was a man, woman or child who came to a living faith in Christ unless the Holy Spirit made Jesus real and winsome to him. You and I cannot do that. We can only construct a neon sign: the Spirit can light it up.

When someone takes the step of faith into Christ and is justified or born again or becomes a new creation or whatever imagery of Christian beginning you prefer, it is the Spirit of God, once again, who takes the initiative. You cannot bring someone from darkness to light. But the Spirit can. You cannot evoke the new creation in his being, but the Spirit can. You cannot baptize him into Christ: only the Spirit can do that. Hence the seven references in the New Testament to people who have been baptized in or with the Holy Spirit (Mk. 1:8; Lk. 3:16; Mt. 3:11; Jn. 1:33; Acts 1:5; 11:16; 1 Cor. 12:13). This explains why Paul is so insistent that no-one can make the most basic Christian confession 'Jesus is Lord', unless the Holy Spirit enables him (1 Cor. 12:3). This is why the whole task of regeneration is ascribed to him (Jn. 3:5). Indeed, if anyone does not have the Spirit of Christ, he is not a Christian (Rom. 8:9). For the Spirit alone can make someone a Christian.

There is a fourth area in Christian beginnings where the Spirit declines to share his glory with another. It is in the whole matter of sealing us into Christ (Eph. 1:13; 4:30) and assuring us that we belong. As mysterious as the secret miracle of new birth is the gentle witness of the Spirit with our spirit that we are indeed children of God; and if children then heirs of God, and fellow heirs with Christ. It is he who whispers in our hearts that we belong, and who enables us to use the first word a Jewish baby would learn to say as he looked into his father's face, 'Abba,' 'Daddy' (Rom. 8:15f.).

We can go further. The whole equipping of the Christian for service is the realm of the Holy Spirit. It is he who distributes spiritual gifts as he thinks fit to different members of Christ's body (1 Cor. 12.7ff.). It is he who enables the lovely fruit of character, which God longs to see, to take root in the barren soil of our lives (Gal. 5:22f.). It is he who changes us from one degree of glory to another until we begin to reflect the beauty of the Lord Jesus. This is entirely the work of the Spirit in us (2 Cor. 3:18).

Wherever we turn, therefore, in this matter of evangelism, we cannot escape our utter and complete dependence on the work and power and witness of the Holy Spirit. He is sovereign. Without him we can effect nothing.

The power of the Spirit in evangelism

How much we need the Holy Spirit in our church life! Has it struck you that if the New Testament is right in marrying up the Holy Spirit with witness-bearing, this might shed a flood of light on the poverty of spiritual experience in many a church and many a Christian? Could it be that we know so little of the Spirit in any powerful way because we care so little for evangelism? Equally, that we know so little of evangelism in

140

any powerful way because we know so little of the Spirit? These two God has joined together, and we cannot put them asunder. No evangelism, no Holy Spirit: no Holy Spirit, no evangelism. There is a vital link between them: and that explains a good deal of the powerlessness in the modern church. The early Christians were well aware that the Holy Spirit and evangelism went together and affected each other intimately. When the Spirit was freely welcomed among them, the outcome was great. In Acts 4:31 we read of a renewed filling of the disciples with the Holy Spirit after a time of heartfelt prayer. In verse 33 we read of the 'great power' which attached to their testimony to Jesus. In the same verse we see that 'great grace' was upon them—and that is not always the case with powerful speakers! Acts 5:5 speaks of the 'great awe' which fell upon people—the deep conviction which only the Spirit can bring. Acts 6:8 faces us with 'great wonders and signs' wrought by Stephen, a man full of the Holy Spirit. And 8:1 discloses that all this produced 'great opposition': it generally does. But 8:8 concludes that there was 'much joy', notwithstanding. Those are some of the great things that happened in the early church when the Spirit had free sway among them. Do we not need that power? Well, it is free, but it will cost us dear. The cost is outlined in five warnings about the Holy Spirit and our reaction to him which are scattered through the pages of the New Testament.

Do not resist the Holy Spirit

That was Stephen's plea to the leaders of Israel (Acts 7:51). It fell on deaf ears. These people were resisting the new move forward by the Holy Spirit in the history of Israel, and this is an ever-present danger for those in Christian leadership. We find it hard to think the Spirit could (or should) do something for the first time. We cling avidly to what we did last year. And if the leadership in any Christian church or movement is bound by the past, they must not be surprised if the new wine cracks the old wineskins and flows elsewhere. There is an uncomfortable regularity with which the church throughout history has resisted movements of reform initiated by the Spirit, or has

141

over-reacted to their errors. The Catholic Church was clearly right to repudiate the charismatic excesses of the Montanist movement at the end of the second century: it was intolerable for people to wander round claiming to be the Holy Spirit! But how tragic that the Montanists were trampled into oblivion. They had an openness to the Spirit, a freedom, a sensitivity to God which was sorely needed in the centuries that followed—but it had been repressed, along with the excesses. It was the same in the days of Wesley, whose enthusiasm seemed such a very horrid thing to the Bishop of London. He was too hot to hold in a lukewarm church, and was driven out. In our own day the American United Methodist Church is not in fellowship with its Wesleyan (and charismatic) sister-church, while the presence of the charismatic 'threat' to the accepted procedure in church has caused many a congregation to ban the movement out of hand. The same is true of many a spiritual movement which makes no claim to be 'charismatic'. In all these respects we are in great danger of following those who stoned Stephen for his dangerous innovations and for following the Spirit, whom he could discern but they could not. If the churches and para-church organizations will not welcome the new life which is so abundantly manifest in almost all the denominations and Christian groups at present—another round of schism may be precipitated. If ministers clamp down too hard and too long on free expressions of spiritual life in their congregations, the lay movement may bypass the clerical bastions of resistance. Do not resist the Holy Spirit.

Do not quench the Holy Spirit

This command to the Thessalonians comes in a context where Paul is talking about the gift of prophecy. He urges them not to quench the Spirit by despising such prophetic manifestations. There are many churches and congregations who would be frightened out of their wits if somebody spoke a word of prophecy in the course of a service. It would be agreed that such a thing must never be allowed to disturb the worship again! And yet the prophets were regarded only slightly less highly than the apostles in the first century, because through them God chose to reveal himself directly to the congregation in encouragement or direction. To be sure, prophecy must be scrutinized. Paul was well aware of the misuse that it could bring. But he did not think that abuse should take away right use. And he laid down in 1 Corinthians 14 a number of wise guidelines for its regulation and testing. There should be only two or three prophecies in a meeting. The longer a prophecy continues the less likely it is to be from God. All should be done in a way that is orderly and honouring to God. And, perhaps most important of all, 'let the others weigh what is said' (1 Cor. 14:29). When God really speaks through a prophecy, the whole congregation has a sense of its rightness and authenticity.

But when all is said, I sense a reluctance in many parts of the Christian church (and these not the parts most characterized by their dynamic life) to accept the possibility that God might use spiritual gifts such as those outlined in 1 Corinthians 12:8–10 or Romans 12:6ff. Helps and administrations would be fine; but not healing, tongues, prophecy or exorcism. It is important to realize that God offers us not only graces of character, such as we read of in Galatians 5:22ff., but powerful gifts as well, which we reject only at our own expense. The Paul who wrote Galatians 5 also wrote 1 Corinthians 12. Happy the church which expects both gifts and graces from the Holy Spirit, and welcomes both alike.

Do not grieve the Holy Spirit

That is Paul's command to the Ephesians (4:30) in a context which suggests that he was thinking of particular sins in their church and individual lives which hurt the Holy Spirit. For the Spirit is like a lover, and is easily hurt, if, as in Ephesus, there are bad relations between husband and wife, malicious and bitter conversations, light fingers prone to steal, unkindness, and filthy talk. In ways like this we very easily grieve the Spirit and rob ourselves of his powerful and gracious working through our lives.

How easily we hurt the Spirit by judging other Christians. Take a trifling example. One of the minor peculiarities in

143

worship among those who like to be called 'charismatic' is the habit of lifting up their arms in worship. On occasion I have been known to do so myself! It happens to be a very ancient and liberating gesture which was used not only in the New Testament (1 Tim. 2:8) but in the later church. In itself it is unimportant. But how zealously some Christians cling to it, however embarrassed others may feel. And how desperately uptight other Christians get about it. 'Emotionalism', they say. Well, most of us have got a long way to go before we show any emotion in our religion, let alone plead guilty to the charge of playing on the emotions! But whenever there is a disagreement about such things, we ought to follow the indications of Romans 14. There we read that some can conscientiously eat meat even if it has been offered to an idol; others are so keen to keep clear of any trace of idolatry that they stick to vegetarian diet. Some scrupulously keep a day special for the Lord, while others, secure in the Lord's liberation, treat all days alike. Christians who differ on these matters are not to criticize or ostracize one another. 'Who are you to pass judgment on the servant of another? It is before his own master that he stands or falls. And he will be upheld, for the Master is able to make him stand,' and Paul concludes the discussion by pointing out that each one shall have to give an account of himself (not of his fellow) to God (Rom. 14:1–12). It is when we start judging one another, criticizing one another, setting an ultimate value on our relative choices, that the Spirit of love and unity is hurt. Do not grieve him.

Do not fear the Spirit

I sometimes detect fear underlying people's criticism of the current emphasis on the Holy Spirit. I sense fear in the hearts of some church members, who are not sure what they would be letting themselves in for if they gave in to the Holy Spirit and allowed him unrestricted access to every side of their lives— emotional lives, business lives, family lives, sexual lives—the lot. I sense fear in the hearts of some ministers who seem afraid that if the Holy Spirit were set free in their congregation, chaos would be let loose: all sorts of lunatics would parade their idiosyncrasies in the name of the Lord, and control would be impossible. After all, how do you shut up someone who thinks he is the mouthpiece of God? And so they are determined that none of this charismatic stuff is to be tolerated in their church. No thank you, not here!

I fully sympathize with both these feelings. I have had them myself. But I am not sure now that they are worthy. I recall that in the Old Testament the Spirit of the Lord is an invading force, the wind of God, reminiscent in sheer power of the sirocco, or the gales whistling down the wadis and ripping up the bushes in their path. I recall that in the New Testament the Spirit is likened to water that inundates parched earth, or fire that burns away until it has destroyed the dross and purified base metal. I think of the 'wind that blows where it likes: so is every one born of the Spirit' (Jn. 3:8). And I have a strong suspicion that the Spirit of Jesus is to be trusted rather than controlled. It is a hard and risky thing to do. On the whole, Catholicism has not trusted him: the Catholic hierarchy have tended to try and confine the Spirit to duly ordered sacraments and ministries over which their church exercises full control. On the whole, the Protestants have not trusted him: Protestant theologians have tried to confine him to a Book over whose exegesis their own researches wield a commanding influence. On the whole, the Pentecostals have not trusted him: control from denominational headquarters is strong and conformity with the cultural *mores* is required.

But the Spirit laughs at our man-made attempts to control him. He is the sovereign Lord God in the midst of us, and he will not be confined. So do not worry that you cannot control him either in your own life or in the congregation. Why should you want to? Is he not wiser than you? Does he not know what he is doing? Remember that the Spirit is the Spirit of Jesus, who is gentle and loving and wants the very best for our lives. Remember that he comes from a Father who gives only good gifts to his children, and will not substitute stones for bread or scorpions for fish. The Lord who is Spirit wants to transform us as individuals and as a church into the likeness of Jesus, and he will only deal violently with us if we violently resist.

But is all this not to give free rein to the lunatic fringe? By no means, granted a wise leadership in the church. Those who claim to have spiritual gifts must allow them to be tested (see p. 143). Moreover, they must back those claims with holiness of life, humility and love if they are to gain a hearing in a church which is by no means persuaded that the Spirit speaks through them. Conversely, those who are dubious about the new enthusiasms, new style of worship and the apparently extravagant claims advanced in the name of the Holy Spirit must also remain open at all costs. It is the work of the Spirit to unite Christ's body, not to divide it. He can and will draw both emphases together, so long as we fulfil our responsibility to 'preserve the unity of the Spirit in the bond of peace'. And that means being open both to the Spirit and to folk with a different emphasis; and it could be that we have something to learn from them!

Do not despise the Holy Spirit

He can give the power we need, and only he.

Power for bearing witness to Jesus. Is that not needed? Are not many Christians tongue-tied at the thought of speaking to anyone else about their Lord, while others find it second nature? The difference lies in the Holy Spirit, and whether or not he has been asked to take over.

Power to cast our fear. Is that not needed? Are many Christians not only speechless about Jesus but crippled with fear and inhibition about launching out in the service of the good news? The perfect love which the Spirit gives casts out fear. Indeed, love is about the only power in the world which is stronger than fear; and love is the first and choicest of the fruits of the Spirit. I have no doubt that Peter was terrified when he found himself, in the earliest days of the church, dragged before a full meeting of the Jewish Sanhedrin, with all the hatchet men of the high priest's family gathered with them, to defend his preaching and healing in the name of the man they had all hated enough to crucify. A very threatening situation. But we read that 'Peter, filled with the Holy Spirit, said to them . . .' (Acts 4:8). The love and power of the Spirit cast out his natural fear. And if you ask the Spirit to fill you, he will do the same for you.

Power to transform character. Is that not needed? And where is it going to come from unless by the agency of the Lord who lives within, the Holy Spirit? The trouble is that although we cannot produce the flowers of character which he is so expert at growing, we can effectively stop his work, by cultivating nettles and brambles. But if he is given full control, the Holy Spirit can impart that bloom, that lustre to our characters which has an intangible but irresistible appeal, and lends a realism to our words about our Lord.

Power for church living. Is that not needed? Many churches are divided in theological emphasis, in social concern or unconcern, by personality cult, by jealousy, by unburied hatchets between church members, by harsh critical judgments on others. Who can impart love? Who can restore unity? Only the Holy Spirit, if he is allowed to sweep in cleansing power into the situation. It is only when we come with our differences and together lay them before the Lord in penitence and ask for His Spirit to bind us together in love—it is only then that the church can get the power to live out its gospel.

Power to love the lost. Do we not need that? Is there not a fog of apathy chilling the hearts of so many of us? Do we really care for others enough to put ourselves out in order to bring them to Christ, with all the praying, the befriending, the expenditure of time and trouble that will involve? No, we do not care enough. You don't and I don't. What is the remedy then? It does not lie with us, but with the Spirit. He gives the power. He imparts the love. And when I come to him and confess my apathy and coldness of heart it is his sovereign work to light and sustain the fires of passionate self-sacrifice in my heart until I begin to feel, to sense again what it was like to be without Christ and without hope in the world. Then, and not till then, am I likely to be stirred out of apathy into service.

Yes, we need the power of the Holy Spirit as we need nothing else. I wonder what you are going to do about it. Because God is not a niggardly donor. He loves to give to those who seek him. It is inconceivable that if you ask for a fuller,

147

deeper experience of his Spirit, he will say you nay. Is he not the heavenly Father who has bidden you ask? You need not add the faithless 'If it is in accordance with your will,' because Scripture makes it abundantly clear that it is in accordance with his will for us to be filled to overflowing with his blessed Holy Spirit. Indeed, it stands in Scripture as a plain, unvarnished command: 'Be filled with the Spirit' (Eph. 5:18). To despise that command is to despise and disobey the God who gave it.

In a word, there are two verses of the New Testament which, I believe, have a particular challenge to us at the end of a study like this. They are Acts 5:32 and Luke 11:13. The first says that God gives his Spirit to those who obey him. The second, 'If you then, who are evil, know how to give good gifts to your children, how much more will your heavenly Father give the Holy Spirit to those who ask him?' *Obey* . . . and *ask*. Those are the conditions for continuing to be filled with the Holy Spirit. The New Testament makes it plain that though baptism with the Holy Spirit is unique and unrepeatable, filling by the Holy Spirit needs often to be repeated and is in fact God's 'standing orders' for us. As we receive from him and give out in service to others, so we need to be filled, and filled and then filled again. But God cannot fill a dirty life and use it in his service; any more than you would fill a dirty cup and use that to quench thirst. The cup must be emptied and washed: only then can it be filled and used. It is like that with us. All sorts of rubbish and dirt gets lodged in our lives. We need to ask the Holy Spirit to cleanse us from even our secret sins—so that although we may not be especially gifted instruments in his service, we may at least be clean. We have to be willing, in a word, to obey, to let God be God in our lives, to have done with anything we know to be wrong, cost what it may. Oh yes, I understand that evil may have become very ingrained from long habit. But it must go if you are to be filled with his Holy Spirit and if you are able to be equipped by that Spirit to share the good news with others. God gives his Spirit to those whose settled determination is to obey him. They may fall; they will fall. But their aim and total direction is to please him in everything. When we are willing to come to that humbling place of recognizing in practical detail the lordship of Christ over our lives, then he will pour upon us his Spirit. We already know the regeneration of the Holy Spirit: we will then discover the 'renewal in the Holy Spirit' which he will pour out upon us richly through Jesus Christ our Saviour (Tit. 3:5–6).

But we have to ask. Those who do not ask do not get: it is evident that they do not really want. We need to ask, and to ask earnestly. We need to go on asking, to go on seeking, to go on knocking, as the Master teaches us in the Sermon on the Mount. Many of us do not sufficiently want the renewing fires of the Holy Spirit to sweep us—at least, not enough to go on asking and seeking and knocking. It would be nice to have the Spirit fill us, but not number-one priority. Why, though, should we think that God will fill us with his number-one gift unless we are willing to make its quest our number-one priority? He does not give his gifts to be trifled with. We need to ask, in earnest.

And we do not need to do anything else. It may help to share with a friend in deep confession and earnest prayer. It may help to have him, or a group of people, lay hands upon you and pray that you may know the fullness of the Spirit. But there is no magic in hands. It may be that you would particularly like the gift of tongues (or particularly wish not to receive it!). Leave the matter to him. He knows how to distribute his gifts where they are needed. He distributes to each Christian severally as he wills. But once we put ourselves unreservedly in his hands, and ask him to take us and fill us and use us in his glorious service—he will do so. There is no prayer that he loves more to answer. And if you feel, 'I have made that dedication and I have asked—but nothing has happened,' I suggest you may have been looking for the wrong thing. The Spirit is not to give you thrills, but to make you Christlike and to fill you with his love and power to witness. I suggest that you leave others to decide whether or not anything has happened; and in the meantime that you thank the heavenly Father for the good gift of his Spirit which he has poured out upon you richly through Jesus Christ your Saviour. And keep thanking him ... and trusting him . . . and pleasing him . . . and witnessing for him as opportunity comes your way. In that way you will find yourself among those who, in their own generation, help to turn the world upside down. You will have begun to put first things first.

A prayer:

> Spirit of the living God, fall afresh on me;
> Spirit of the living God, fall afresh on me.
> Break me, cleanse me, fill me, use me.
> Spirit of the living God, fall afresh on me.

THE WEST 34

CHRISTIAN MIND 50 F

MAJOR EMPHASIS 52